THE ASCENSION

Lenten Companion

Walking with Jesus to Jerusalem

Fr. Mark Toups

ASCENSION

West Chester, Pennsylvania

Ascension
PO Box 1990
West Chester, PA 19380
1-800-376-0520
ascensionpress.com

ISBN: 978-1-954882-43-0 (paperback)
ISBN: 978-1-954882-44-7 (e-book)

CONTENTS

GETTING THE MOST OUT OF
THE ASCENSION LENTEN COMPANION

The book you have in your hands is the first of a new trilogy of *Lenten Companion* journals from Ascension that follow Jesus on his journey to Jerusalem. It aims to help you draw closer to Jesus Christ through daily reflections and guided prayers.

The journal is meant to be used with video presentations by Fr. Toups, which are freely available at **ascensionpress.com/lentencompanion**. The videos and journals are ideal for parishes, small groups, and individuals to use during Lent.

Community

Community is a key component of the journey to holiness. Lent provides an excellent opportunity to spend more time in prayer and strengthen friendships with others on the shared journey to heaven.

The ideal is for a whole parish to take up the *Lenten Companion* and journey together as a community. The *Lenten Companion* journal and videos are designed to be used by parishes, small groups, and individuals in preparation for Easter. You can find out how to provide journals to a large parish group at **ascensionpress.com/lentencompanion**, which also includes information about buying in bulk and running parish events with the *Lenten Companion* videos and journal.

If you cannot experience the *Lenten Companion* as a whole parish, consider a small group setting. Use the *Lenten Companion* as a family devotion for Lent, or get together with a few friends to discuss how God is speaking to you during this season. Bulk pricing for small groups is also available.

The *Lenten Companion* is also well suited to use by individuals. Remember that you are not alone—Catholics all over the country are on the same journey. This journal is meant to provide a place for you to speak with God and to hear and see everything he wants to show you.

Videos

To accompany the journal, the *Lenten Companion* offers videos with Fr. Mark Toups. Through his witness, conversation, and prayer, you will find fresh insights into the profound love the Lord pours out for us on the Cross.

The eight videos are for Ash Wednesday, the five weeks of Lent, Holy Week, and the Triduum. These videos are available on DVD and can likewise be viewed at **ascensionpress.com/lentencompanion**.

Daily Meditations

Each day, a new reflection invites you to listen to God's voice as you walk with Jesus to Jerusalem for his Passion, death, and resurrection. The meditation begins with a word to orient your prayer and a brief passage from Scripture. The day's reflection closes with a prompt titled "For Your Prayer" and lines for journaling to help you open your heart to the Lord.

Weekly Reflections and Discussion Questions

At the end of each week, we invite you to review the week's meditations and journal about your experience. We include three questions at the end of each Saturday meditation to help with this. Many people will find it fruitful to discuss the questions when they meet with others in their parish or small group; you can also ponder them on your own. Use these questions to reflect on your experience throughout the week—with the video presentation, the daily meditations, and your journal entries. Notice how your prayer might change, and write about the things that have touched you most profoundly during the week.

Approaching Prayer

As you dedicate yourself to prayer this Lent, there is no better safeguard than a good plan. We recommend using the five Ws to make a plan. Here's how they work: Every Sunday, look at your calendar and write your plan for the next six days. Make the plan specific by answering the five W questions—When? Where? What? Who? Why?

> WHEN will I spend time with Jesus?
>
> WHERE will I spend time with Jesus?
>
> WHAT are Jesus and I going to do together?
>
> WHO will hold me accountable for my time with Jesus?
>
> WHY am I prioritizing my time with Jesus?

With your plan in place, you may find these steps helpful when praying with Scripture and other texts:

Prepare

Read the text once to get familiar with the words. If you are praying imaginatively, read through the whole scene. Then slowly read the text a second time. Pay attention to how you feel as you read. Notice which words strike you. If the text sets a scene, enter it with the people mentioned. Imagine the scene in as much detail as possible.

Sometimes it helps to read the passage a third time. Enter it fully, lingering with it until it feels right to move on.

Acknowledge

You have read the text. You have entered the scene. Now *acknowledge* what stirs within you. Pay attention to your thoughts, feelings, and desires. They are important.

Relate

When you have acknowledged what is going on inside your heart, *relate* that to God. Don't just think about your questions, feelings, and desires. Don't just think about God or how God might react. Tell him how you feel. Tell him what you think. Tell him what you want. Share all your thoughts with him.

Receive

When you have shared everything with God, it's time to *receive* from him. Listen to what he is telling you. It could be a subtle voice you hear. It could be a memory that pops up. Maybe he invites you to reread the Scripture passage. Perhaps he invites you into a still, restful silence. Trust that God is listening to you, and receive what he wants to share with you. Stay here for as long as you desire.

Respond

Now *respond*. Your response could be continuing your conversation with God or resolving to do something. It could be tears or laughter. Respond to what you are receiving.

Journal

The last step is to journal. Keep a record of what your prayer is like. Your journal entry does not have to be lengthy. It can be a single word or sentence about what God told you or how the day's meditation struck you. No matter how you do it, journaling will help you walk more intentionally with God this Lent. We have provided space for you to journal every day and at the end of every week.

Commit

Making a commitment is the first step in transforming your prayer life. This season with *The Lenten Companion: Walking with Jesus to Jerusalem* is your perfect chance to begin.

Introduction

Imagine getting ready for a walking trip, such as the Camino de Santiago or a long hike. You have the essentials for the trip already figured out: a water bottle, good hiking shoes, sunscreen, a sturdy walking stick. Just before you set out, you dig through your knapsack one last time to decide what possessions you can afford to leave behind (you can't take on the extra weight when you have to carry everything). You know what your general destination is—you've been there before—but you are not very familiar with the trail you will be taking to get there this time. Thankfully, you know of a guide you can trust who is very familiar with the route. They are willing to walk by your side every step of the way, helping you through challenging stretches and highlighting the beautiful parts. All you have to do is follow their lead.

On Ash Wednesday, you will embark on a forty-day journey of your own: Lent.

You know the essentials you will need to prepare for this Lenten journey: prayer, fasting, and almsgiving. There will be parts of your life such as distractions, habits, and small comforts that you may choose to "take out of your knapsack" and give up for the next forty days. While the destination for Lent (Easter Sunday) is familiar to you, the specific route you are going to take to get there this year will be new for you. Thankfully, there is someone who can guide you—someone who has not only undertaken this journey before, but who also wants to be at your side through every challenge and beautiful moment of Lent: Jesus himself.

In some ways, this book can serve as your travel journal. Each day you will walk with Jesus as he heads to Jerusalem, and you will have the chance to pause and reflect on each stage of his journey. You will be able to meet those who also walked with him, those who were pierced to the heart by his words or who were disturbed by his teachings. Each week you will be able to look back over how far you've come and the lessons you've learned on the way. The further you go on this path, the more challenges you will encounter, both in Scripture and in yourself. The key to it all is, in a word, trust.

Ask yourself now: Will you allow Jesus to guide you on this journey? Will you follow him even when he guides you away from your comfort zone and closer to the parts of your life that need healing? Will you listen to him when he asks you to leave behind familiar territory and challenges you to go deeper than you have ever gone? Will you rely on him even when your path takes you straight to the Cross?

As you begin this Lenten journey, be encouraged by the fact that you can trust in your guide completely. He is looking forward to taking this journey alongside you. His greatest hope is that this time of Lent will bring you closer together. All you have to do is follow his lead.

It's time for the journey to begin. It starts with two simple words:

"Follow me."

Determined

Person

*"Then Jesus told his disciples,
'If any man would come after me, let him deny
himself and take up his cross and follow me.'"*

—MATTHEW 16:24

Ash Wednesday

In the first paragraph of his first encyclical, Pope Benedict XVI writes, "Being Christian is not the result of an ethical choice or a lofty idea, but the encounter with an event, *a person*, which gives life a new horizon and a decisive direction."[1] The piercing simplicity of these words is deeply moving.

Being Christian is not about me. Being Christian is not about my choice for God. Being Christian cannot be defined by rules or rituals, nor can it be summed up in policies or piety. Of course, all these things are a part of the "holy order" of Catholicism. But being Christian is essentially about a person—and his name is Jesus.

Christianity is about *Jesus, a person.* It has been this way from the beginning. When Jesus called his disciples, his invitation was "Follow *me*" (Matthew 4:19; Luke 5:27; John 1:43, emphasis added). When he taught them the truth, he explicitly said, "*I* am the way, and the truth, and the life; no one comes to the Father but by *me*" (John 14:6, emphasis added). No other religious leader in history has intentionally placed the focus on himself. However, Jesus continually places himself at the center of faith.

When we encounter this person, our lives change. Peter, a simple fisherman, was a seasoned master at reading nature and people; his life changed because he encountered a *person*. Mary Magdalene was a wounded soul possessed by demons; her life changed because she encountered a *person*. The lives of sinners, outcasts, the ignored, and the forgotten were transformed because they encountered a *person*. For each of them, "the encounter with an event, *a person*," gave life "a new horizon and a decisive direction."

If Christianity is about a person, that means Lent is also about a person. Lent is not simply about prayer, fasting, and almsgiving.

Those disciplines help us focus on what we need to focus on: namely, *a person*. Lent is about a person. Lent is about Jesus.

I invite you today to join me on a journey. Over the next forty-six days, we will spend our lives with a *person*. We will eat with him, walk with him, and laugh with him. We will listen to his words of mercy and witness sinners' hearts transformed. We will see him push boundaries and expand our understanding of love. We will feel the liberation of those who were bound and taste the shock of the religious authorities. We will come to love this person, Jesus, who will ultimately be betrayed, imprisoned, tortured, and crucified.

This is your invitation. This is your Lent. Welcome to the journey. Welcome to the encounter with a *person* who gives life "a new horizon and a decisive direction."

For Your Prayer

After reading today's meditation, stay here in this prayerful place for another ten minutes. In silence, ask yourself, "What do I really want from God this Lent?" Then close your eyes and, in the silence, tell the Lord what you want from him this season.

What words stood out to you as you prayed?
What did you find stirring in your heart?

Determined

"When the days for his being taken up were fulfilled, he resolutely determined to journey to Jerusalem."

—LUKE 9:51 NAB

Today we begin with the Gospel of Luke. Throughout Lent, our meditations will primarily focus on Luke's presentation of Jesus' epic journey to Jerusalem.

Luke 9 is of critical importance. Jesus sends out the Twelve with authority "over all demons" (Luke 9:1). He feeds more than five thousand people (Luke 9:10–17), and Peter acknowledges that Jesus is indeed the long-awaited Messiah (Luke 9:18–21). Then the story shifts as Jesus confesses that the "Son of Man must suffer many things, and be rejected by the elders and chief priests, and the scribes, and be killed" (Luke 9:22).

Now, after Jesus' Transfiguration, "when the days for his being taken up were fulfilled, he resolutely determined to journey to Jerusalem" (Luke 9:51 NAB). The journey begins. Jesus is determined. Knowing that his Passion and death await him at the end of his journey, Jesus is "resolutely determined" to start.

What does it mean to be "resolutely determined?" The word *resolute* implies being steady and unwavering in love, allegiance, or conviction. The word *determined* implies being bound to a purpose, mission, or person. To be "resolutely determined" means being bound out of allegiance or love. Jesus is bound in love for the Father. It is the *Person* of the Father who forges the resolute determination of Jesus.

For many of us, Lent is a time when we adopt Lenten penances and special commitments to God so that we may grow in holiness. But far too often, our Lenten penances take the shape of our New Year's resolutions: we mean well at the beginning, but when life gets busy, our determination atrophies, and we give up.

Just as Jesus' resolute determination was forged by his relationship with the Father, we are shaped by our commitment to a *person*. Regardless of where you are in your relationship with Jesus, how well you know him, or how many questions you have about him, he is inviting you to follow him this Lent.

Imagine for a moment that Jesus is looking at you right now. He is asking, "Will you follow me? Will you stay with me? Are you determined to go with me all the way to Jerusalem?"

For Your Prayer

Stay here for an additional ten minutes. Pray with Luke 9:18–22 and 9:51. Be present in the scene. Be there with Jesus. Ask the Holy Spirit to help you see what the people in the Gospel saw and hear what they heard. Let the scene unfold in your imagination as it does in the Bible. Then, at the end of the scene, imagine that Jesus looks at you. Jesus asks you, "Are you resolutely determined to follow me all the way to Jerusalem?"

What words stood out to you as you prayed?
What did you find stirring in your heart?

_____

_____

_____

_____

_____

_____

_____

_____

_____

_____

_____

_____

_____

_____

_____

_____

_____

_____

_____

_____

_____

_____

_____

_____

Open

"Make ready for him."

—LUKE 9:52

As Jesus begins his journey to Jerusalem, so too do all those who are with him. We read in Luke 9:52, "He sent messengers ahead of him, who went and entered a village of the Samaritans, to make ready for him." Jesus is making his way to Samaria, and while he is there, he hopes the people will be open to receiving all that he has to share with them. Thus, he sends followers in advance to "make ready for him."

Jesus' messengers are tasked with making provision for his arrival. This includes practical things such as food and water, lodging, and a place to teach. However, it also involves more personal matters, such as speaking to Samaritans.

In Jesus' day, Samaritans and Jews had nothing to do with each other. Their animosity was rooted in divisions that occurred centuries before—so Jesus' decision to enter Samaria would have caused quite a stir. The Samaritans would have had many questions for the messengers sent to prepare Jesus' way. Above all, they would have wanted to know what Jesus would do and say.

The beginning of our journey to Jerusalem coincides with the start of another journey: Lent. As one who will walk with you on the journey, I ask you to think about how, together, we can prepare for Jesus.

The Samaritans would have asked, "What will he do and say?" You are probably wondering the same thing. So am I. We can begin by admitting that we do not know.

You may be a veteran of Lent. You may have even read other *Ascension Lenten Companion* books. You may think that there is nothing more Jesus can do and say. Well, just as no one knew exactly what Jesus was going to do and say back then, you do not know what he has in store for you this Lent either. I ask you to be open. Be present in the present moment. Let go of your expectations. Let Jesus do and say what he wants. Jesus is the one who has invited you on this journey to Jerusalem.

Lent is as much an encounter as it is a liturgical season. Lent is an encounter with Jesus. While we may be encountering the same person, we—*you*—are certainly not the same person having the encounter. Because of your experiences and growth, you are different now than last year or during any Lent in the past. Jesus' love for you is unique, and Jesus seeks to love you within the particular circumstances of your life as it is now.

You have never been here, now, as you are now. So, I'll say again: be open to him. Be in the present moment. Let go of your expectations. Let Jesus do and say what he wants.

For Your Prayer

Stay here for an additional ten minutes. Today pray with Jeremiah 29:11–14. Trust the one who is speaking to you through these words and give him permission to lead you.

What words stood out to you as you prayed?
What did you find stirring in your heart?

_____

_____

_____

_____

_____

_____

_____

_____

_____

_____

_____

_____

_____

_____

_____

_____

_____

_____

_____

_____

_____

_____

Follow

"Follow me."

—LUKE 9:59

As we walk with Jesus on his journey to Jerusalem, we hear Jesus say two words that have changed people's lives for more than two thousand years: "Follow me."

To follow someone means to pay attention to where they are going and what they are doing. Sometimes we follow someone because we do not know the way to our destination. Sometimes we follow because we know one way to get there, but someone else knows a better way. Both reasons apply to us this Lent.

I mentioned to you yesterday that while you may have been through Lent before, you have never been through *this* Lent at this stage of your life and in the particular circumstances you are facing. Following Jesus, letting him lead you, assures you that you will arrive at your desired destination.

However, the one we are following also desires to know where we want to go. In a sense, Jesus is asking you today, "What do you want this Lent? What do you need? Where are you in life? What do you ask of me?" Jesus seeks to take you on a journey within. Therefore, naming your desires at the beginning of the journey will dispose you to receive from him the deepest desires of your heart.

Jesus says, "Follow *me*." There is a *me* to follow. We don't so much follow a map or a route; we follow a person. When we do so, we discover that the journey is as important as the destination, if not more so. The journey to Jerusalem will entail much more than merely arriving there. The journey is about Jesus and what he's doing along the way. It's about how the journey prepares us for the destination. It's about what happens to us—and within us—while we are on the journey.

As we round out the initial days of Lent and prepare to enter the first full week of our journey, take some time today to tell the Lord what you desire. Tell him what your heart longs for during this season. Then, to conclude, pray the *Suscipe* Prayer from St. Ignatius of Loyola:

"Take, Lord, and receive all my liberty, my memory, my understanding, and my entire will, all that I have and possess. Thou hast given all to me. To Thee, O Lord, I return it. All is Thine, dispose of it wholly according to Thy will. Give me Thy love and Thy grace, for this is sufficient for me."[2]

For Your Prayer

Stay here for an additional ten minutes. Today pray with Luke 18:35–42. Be present in the scene. You are the blind man. Ask the Holy Spirit to help you be in the place of the man begging. Imagine that Jesus looks at you and says, "What do you want me to do for you?" What do you say? What do you desire from God?

What words stood out to you as you prayed?
What did you find stirring in your heart?

_____

_____

_____

_____

_____

_____

_____

_____

_____

_____

_____

_____

_____

_____

_____

_____

_____

_____

_____

_____

_____

_____

H ere are three questions to help you reflect on this week's meditations. You may find it helpful to discuss them with others or ponder them on your own before you begin the weekly reflection:

- As we explored this week, Lent is an encounter with a person—Jesus—and no matter how many Lents you have experienced, you are a different person now than you were in previous years. What unique experiences from the past year are you carrying into this Lenten journey? Where is the Lord coming to meet you as we begin?

- Please return to the definitions of *resolute* and *determined* that we broke down on p. 9. This season, Jesus asks us: "Are you *resolutely determined* to follow me to Jerusalem?" What practical things can you do to help yourself commit to this journey over the next five weeks? In what ways can you daily accept Jesus' invitation to follow him?

- **VIDEO REFLECTION:** What did you think about the story of the old man feeding the birds? In what ways does the man's response to the two boys relate to your experience and journey with Jesus this Lent?

Now take a moment to reflect on the past week, going over the meditations that bore the most fruit in your prayer, the things you wrote, and your reflections on this week's video. How has your prayer changed this week?

Transformed

Love

"You shall love the Lord your God
with all your heart,
and with all your soul,
and with all your strength,
and with all your mind;
and your neighbor as yourself."

—LUKE 10:27

The more time we spend with someone, the more we get to know them. We hear what they say, and we want to know why they say it. We become fascinated by their thoughts. We come to know their history. We come to know what is important to them.

If we think about falling in love, we realize this is the pattern of ordinary relationships. The "falling" in love is an experience of becoming fascinated with someone other than ourselves. The architecture of our souls is such that we were made to transcend ourselves. We were made for another.

Let us imagine for a moment what happened in the lives of Peter and Mary Magdalene. Both spent time with Jesus—a lot of time. They not only listened to him as he spoke to the crowds, but they both had sacred time alone with him. They heard what he said and became more and more fascinated with why he said it. They came to know his thoughts, his history, what was important to him. They came to know love.

When we spend time with Jesus, one thing becomes clear: *love*. Jesus *is* love. Jesus revealed love. He spoke of love and showed love and responded out of love. Everything that he did, everything that he was, was about love. Jesus radiated love. Jesus was motivated by love. This epic journey toward Jerusalem is about one thing: *love*.

Along the journey, as Jesus was teaching, "a lawyer stood up to put him to the test, saying, 'Teacher, what shall I do to inherit eternal life?' He said to him, 'What is written in the law? What do you read there?' And he answered, 'You shall love the Lord your God with all your heart, and with all your soul, and with all your strength, and with all your mind; and your neighbor as yourself.' And he said to him, 'You have answered right; do this, and you will live'" (Luke 10:25-28). The story doesn't end here, but let's pause now to focus on what Jesus just said.

What is love? Pope Benedict XVI in *Deus Caritas Est* wrote, "God's love for us is fundamental for our lives, and it raises important questions about who God is and who we are. In considering this, we immediately find ourselves hampered by a problem of language. Today, the term 'love' has become one of the most frequently used and misused of words, a word to which we attach quite different meanings."[3] Despite modern language problems, St. Thomas Aquinas' definition of love is tried and true: "To love is to will the good of the other."[4]

We often experience *feelings* of love, but love is not merely a feeling. Love is something you *do*. This journey to Jerusalem is all about love. It will motivate Jesus, captivate sinners, and be too much for some scribes and Pharisees.

For Your Prayer

Stay here for an additional ten minutes. Today pray with 1 Corinthians 13:1–7. As you read, consider how these words describe the way Jesus loves you. Spend some time with Jesus. Talk to him about love.

What words stood out to you as you prayed?
What did you find stirring in your heart?

Inflated

"*I came that they may have life,
and have it abundantly.*"

—JOHN 10:10

Why did Jesus come? Why Christmas and the Incarnation? Why Lent, Holy Week, and Easter? Why are we walking together on this epic journey to Jerusalem?

We live in a world obsessed with diversion: we long for the weekend, we anticipate our vacation, we relish fantasy. But is that the way it is supposed to be? To understand Jesus, to understand this journey, we have to understand that our lives here on earth are not "as good as it gets."

In his book *Theology of the Body Explained,* Christopher West writes, "Without reference to God's original plan and its hope of restoration in Christ, people tend to accept discord ... 'as just the way it is.'"[5] Sound familiar? If we all think this life is "as good as it gets," perhaps we're missing something and don't even know it. West continues, "When we normalize our fallen state, it is akin to thinking it normal to drive with flat tires. We intuit that something is amiss, but when everyone drives around in the same state, we lack a point of reference for anything different."[6]

I love that image. Think about it: your heart, your life, is the "tires." Perfect union with God, his love for us and our love for him, is the air for our tires. In God's original plan, we lived in communion with him and were filled with God's love; our tires were filled.

Your life is supposed to be full of joy, peace, and love. In the Gospel of John, we read, "I came that they may have life, and have it abundantly" (John 10:10). He also says to us, "These things I have spoken to you, that my joy may be in you, and that your joy may be full" (John 15:11). This is what God wants for you. God longs for each of us to be filled with love.

This is what happened in the lives of Peter and Mary Magdalene. They came to know Jesus personally, and their lives were forever changed. They came to know love and Jesus' longing for love. In Jesus, with Jesus, and because of Jesus, their hearts were inflated. They were filled with love.

The question is this: How are your tires? Are they inflated or flat? Do you think this life is as good as it gets? Are you hungry for more in life? If so, what exactly do you hunger for? This Lent, what do you *really* want from God?

For Your Prayer

Stay here for an additional ten minutes. Today pray with Psalm 63 or Psalm 42 (or both). As you read, consider that these very words are words Jesus himself would have prayed.

What words stood out to you as you prayed?
What did you find stirring in your heart?

Flat

"I stretch out my hands to you; my soul thirsts for you like a parched land."

—PSALM 143:6

In God's original plan, Adam and Eve enjoyed perfect communion in the Garden of Eden. Their lives were filled with love—perfect love.

The icon of this perfect love is found in marriage. In the beginning, Adam and Eve enjoyed a perfect marriage with each other (Genesis 2:24–25). And what was true of their marriage was true because of their relationship with God; Adam and Eve had a perfect marriage because there existed a perfect marriage between God and humanity.

But Genesis 2 is followed by Genesis 3; the Creation is followed by the Fall. In Genesis 2, God's perfect love fills all creation. In Genesis 3, God's original plan is disrupted. The communion between Adam and Eve, and between God and humanity, is broken. To return to Christopher West's analogy about tires, these once "inflated" relationships become flat.

Because of the Fall, all creation has been torn away from perfect union with God. Now, thanks to the reality of sin, everyone drives with flat tires—and we sometimes forget this isn't how life is supposed to be. I can recall countless times in my own life when I wanted more and asked myself, "Am I happy? Am I *really* happy?" I can recall countless times when I said to others, "There has to be more to life than this."

In such moments, life seems empty. Our hearts long for more. I know firsthand what this is like.

How would you describe your life, your heart? Are you tired? Have you believed the lie that this life is "as good as it gets"? What are you hungry for? Here are a few indications that you might be living with flat tires:

- You are constantly thinking about the next thing: the next vacation, the next diversion, the next distraction.

- You need more and more of what you have just to experience the same level of satisfaction.

- You live with a quiet fear of missing out. You are constantly looking at what *could* be happening in your life rather than what *is* happening in your life.

- Although other people may not know it, you have some form of addiction. There is a pattern of your life which, even if you wanted to, you could not stop (e.g., pornography, spending, drinking).

- You can remember a time when you were happy. But you are no longer as happy as you were then. You are longing for more. You are longing to be happy.

What if Jesus could change your life and restore your joy, peace, and love? What if Jesus could do for you that which he did for all those people who were with him on his journey to Jerusalem? Would you want that? What do you want? What do you *really* want?

For Your Prayer

Stay here for an additional ten minutes. Today pray with Isaiah 55. As you read, consider that these very words are words Jesus himself would have prayed.

What words stood out to you as you prayed?
What did you find stirring in your heart?

_____

_____

_____

_____

_____

_____

_____

_____

_____

_____

_____

_____

_____

_____

_____

_____

_____

_____

_____

_____

_____

_____

_____

_____

_____

_____

_____

Restore

"For God so loved the world that he gave his only-begotten Son, that whoever believes in him should not perish but have eternal life."

—JOHN 3:16

L et us return to Christopher West: "Without reference to God's original plan and its hope of restoration in Christ, people tend to accept discord ... 'as just the way it is.'"[7] If we really believe that we are supposed to live with flat tires, life becomes nothing more than simply chasing one thing after another. We may be tempted to live on the hamster wheel of diversion, distraction, and the pursuit of pleasure. However, Jesus invites us to more.

So, I ask again: Why did Jesus come? Why Christmas and the Incarnation? Why Lent, Holy Week, and Easter? Why are we walking together on this epic journey to Jerusalem? Because "God so loved the world that he gave his only-begotten Son, so that whoever believes in him should not perish but have eternal life" (John 3:16).

Jesus came so we could live in the fullness of God's love. In the beginning, perfect love filled the world, and all humankind was married to God. Because of the Fall, we lost that perfect marriage and perfect love. "Flat tires" became the norm.

Jesus, however, comes to *restore* what was lost. Jesus comes to wed humanity back to God. He comes to restore all creation to the communion with God that Adam and Eve once enjoyed in the Garden. That's why we are on this journey. That's why Jesus came. That's why he is determined to make it to Jerusalem: to love, to restore creation, to restore your life.

Let us review the last four days. Jesus is love. Throughout this epic journey to Jerusalem, we will come to see just how far he will go to love us. Jesus came because of the reality of the Fall. Because of the Fall, the perfect marriage between God and humanity was broken. Now, we all drive around with flat tires.

On our journey to Jerusalem, we will see thousands of people who flock to Jesus because of the reality of living broken lives. Like them, we get tired of living with flat tires. We sense that there is more to life than flat tires. And every once in a while, we get tired of being tired. We will meet many people in the coming weeks who, like us, are hungry for more.

During this journey to Jerusalem, we will also see how Jesus' message of love and mercy pushes the boundaries of many people's expectations and accepted beliefs—bringing hope to some, bewildering others, and enraging a select few, including the scribes and Pharisees. Looking through the lens of an angry righteousness, those who are most hostile to Jesus will be unable to recognize the Messiah in their midst.

For Your Prayer

Stay here for an additional ten minutes. Today pray with Psalm 37:1–7 and consider the following: What if Jesus could change your life and restore your joy, peace, and love? What if Jesus could do for you what he did for all those people who were with him on his journey to Jerusalem? Would you want that? What do you really want?

What words stood out to you as you prayed?
What did you find stirring in your heart?

_____

_____

_____

_____

_____

_____

_____

_____

_____

_____

_____

_____

_____

_____

_____

_____

_____

_____

_____

_____

_____

_____

Bridegroom

"As the bridegroom rejoices over the bride,
so shall your God rejoice over you."

—ISAIAH 62:5

In this first week of Lent, we are laying a foundation on which we can build a more personal understanding of who Jesus is and what will unfold during this journey to Jerusalem. This week we have come to appreciate Jesus and his love for us, a love which seeks to restore us, to inflate our flat tires. We lost the air in our tires when the perfect marriage between God and humanity was fractured in the Fall. This means that to understand Jesus and his journey to Jerusalem, we must also understand how he is coming to fix this great divorce.

While many Jews were awaiting a Messianic king (2 Samuel 7:12), the remnant core of Israel was awaiting the Bridegroom-Messiah who would wed humanity with God. In both Isaiah 54 and 62, we read of God's desire to be united with his people in abiding love.

The Bible itself is filled with references to marriage. It starts with the marriage of Adam and Eve (Genesis 2:24) and ends with the marriage of the Lamb and his Bride (Revelation 21:2). Close the Bible and find the exact middle of the Scriptures—the Song of Songs, the love poem between the Bride and Bridegroom.

In his 1994 *Letter to Families*, St. John Paul II wrote that "by describing himself as a Bridegroom, Jesus reveals the essence of God and confirms his immense love for mankind." In doing so, "he indicated the fulfillment in his own person of the image of God the Bridegroom, which had already been used in the Old Testament, in order to fully reveal the mystery of God as the mystery of love."[8]

During this journey to Jerusalem, Jesus is inviting you into his heart. It is a heart burning with love. It is not abstract or general or sterile. As the love of a husband for his wife, a bridegroom for his bride, the love he has is a personal love.

Jesus loves you in this very particular way. He does not see you as he sees everyone else; he sees *you*. He sees the very distinct *you* that you are. He sees your needs and the ways you resist his love. He loves you with great passion and without limits. Jesus' passionate, limitless love is what propels him to the Cross.

Someone once said to me that we all need love, and we all need more than we deserve. The good news for you is that regardless of where you are in your relationship with Jesus, he is pursuing you. Jesus is pursuing you with a very personal and passionate love. You do not have to earn it. All you have to do is receive it.

Let him find you. Be open to all he desires to give you in this season of Lent. Ask for what you need. Trust in his desire for you.

For Your Prayer

Stay here for an additional ten minutes. Today pray with Isaiah 54:4–8. Be attentive to how these words were inspired by God to specifically describe Jesus.

What words stood out to you as you prayed?
What did you find stirring in your heart?

_____
_____
_____
_____
_____
_____
_____
_____
_____
_____
_____
_____
_____
_____
_____
_____
_____
_____
_____
_____
_____
_____
_____

"You have answered right; do this, and you will live."

—LUKE 10:28

We have seen that Jesus is love and that this entire journey to Jerusalem is an act of love. You and I were made for love: when we look at the story of Creation in Genesis 1, we see that our hearts were made to be filled with God's abiding love. Unfortunately, because of the Fall and the consequences of Original Sin, our experience of life feels flat. All humanity needs restoration, and the only one who can reconcile us back to God is God himself. This is how we are to understand the Person of Jesus and the reason we are on this journey to Jerusalem.

Jesus as the Bridegroom-Messiah has come to wed humanity back to God. Jesus has come to bring all of us back into an intimate communion with the Trinity. This is what love is, and this is what love does. Love is something you do, not merely something you feel.

On Sunday we looked at the story of Jesus' conversation with the lawyer who wants to inherit eternal life. When prompted, the lawyer responds to Jesus by quoting the heart of Mosaic Law: "You shall love the Lord your God with all your heart, and with all your soul, and with all your strength, and with all your mind; and your neighbor as yourself." To that, Jesus responds, "You have answered right; do this, and you will live" (Luke 10:25–28).

Do this. That is what Jesus says to him: "Do this." Again, love is something we *do.*

How can we best understand how Jesus himself loves? If we understand Jesus as the Bridegroom-Messiah, then the Rite of Matrimony gives us something to consider. Before the exchange of vows, for example, couples are asked, "Have you come here to enter into Marriage without coercion, freely and wholeheartedly?"[9] Jesus would respond, "Yes." And in John 10:17–18, he says, "I lay down my life, that I may take it again. No one takes it from me, but I lay it down of my own accord. I have power to lay it down, and I have power to take it again." There is no coercion. Jesus is free. Freely and wholeheartedly, he gives himself to us.

In the exchange of vows, the spouses say, "I promise to be faithful to you, in good times and in bad, in sickness and in health, to love you and to honor you all the days of my life."[10] This too is applicable to Jesus. Jesus is *always* faithful to us. Regardless of how we may struggle in our relationship with him, Jesus is always faithful. He is there "in good times and in bad." He is with us "in sickness and in health." In both our physical and spiritual sickness, Jesus is there. At all times, in every moment of life, Jesus is forever loving us.

For Your Prayer

Stay here for an additional ten minutes. Today pray with Isaiah 62:1–5. Be attentive to how these words were inspired by God to specifically describe Jesus.

What words stood out to you as you prayed?
What did you find stirring in your heart?

_____

_____

_____

_____

_____

_____

_____

_____

_____

_____

_____

_____

_____

_____

_____

_____

_____

_____

_____

_____

_____

Everything

"All your strength."

—LUKE 10:27

Today as we wrap up this first week of Lent, I would like to lead you in a guided meditation. Let us ask the Holy Spirit to inspire us as we pray. May the Holy Spirit awaken our spiritual senses so that we may enter the scene and see what those in the Gospel saw, hear what they heard, and feel what they felt.

Imagine that you are with Jesus and a small crowd of people sitting outside a small synagogue in a small town in Israel. Take a few moments to picture the surroundings: the arid land, the stone buildings, and the simple structures of the poor town. You can see it all in your imagination, especially Jesus. Peace radiates from his presence. He is calm and composed. He is confident.

Imagine that you are sitting with Jesus as the scene in Luke 10 unfolds. You are with Jesus when a man, a lawyer, stands up. With a confrontational look on his face, he approaches Jesus, seeking to prove something. He stops in front of Jesus. All eyes are on him, anticipating what is about to happen. He says to Jesus, "Teacher, what shall I do to inherit eternal life?"

Jesus also stands. With great love, Jesus looks the man directly in the eyes and says to him, "What is written in the law? What do you read there?" Very quickly, the lawyer responds to Jesus, saying, "You shall love the Lord your God with all your heart, and with all your soul, and with all your strength, and with all your mind; and your neighbor as yourself." Watch Jesus as he replies: "You have answered right; do this, and you will live."

People linger for a while. But now imagine a moment when everyone else has left the area, and it is just the two of you, you and Jesus. Jesus looks you in the eye and says to you, "Do you know how much I love you?" You are silent, not expecting such a question. But you want to ponder it before you give an answer. What is in your heart as he asks you this question? There is no right answer other than your answer. What do you want to say to Jesus as he asks you this?

Now imagine that Jesus says to you, "I love you with all my heart and with all my soul and with all my strength and with all my mind. As I have asked others to love this way, this is how *I* love. I love with *everything*. I hold nothing back. I hold nothing back from you. I love you."

Pause for a moment and consider who is speaking to you. Consider the very words he is saying. Jesus loves you with all his heart. How big is his heart? How much is the "all" that Jesus is able to love you with? How strong is God? When he loves you with all his strength, how strong is that love?

Stay in the moment and let Jesus' words wash over your heart. Jesus loves you this much. Allow yourself to receive these words.

For Your Prayer

Stay here for an additional ten minutes. Today close your eyes and imagine the scene above.

What words stood out to you as you prayed?
What did you find stirring in your heart?

_____

_____

_____

_____

_____

_____

_____

_____

_____

_____

_____

_____

_____

_____

_____

_____

_____

_____

_____

H ere are three questions to help you reflect on this week's meditations. You may find it helpful to discuss them with others or ponder them on your own before you begin the weekly reflection:

- Return to the list on p. 34. What bullet point(s) do you relate to the most right now? What struggle is Jesus asking you to surrender to him this Lent so that he may fill you up again?

- As we mentioned earlier this week, Jesus loves *you* personally, intimately, with all his strength. He particularly loves that which makes you *you*: your humor, your quirks, your spirit, your whole self. Thinking about just how specific and individual his love is for you, what thoughts and feelings come to mind?

- **VIDEO REFLECTION:** How does picturing Jesus as a Bridegroom affect your understanding of his mission and his journey to Jerusalem? How does it affect the way you see your relationship with Jesus?

Now take a moment to reflect on the past week, going over the meditations that bore the most fruit in your prayer, the things you wrote, and your reflections on this week's video. How has your prayer changed this week?

Mercy

Deeper

"Jesus replied ... "

—LUKE 10:30

L ast week we explored Luke 10 and steeped ourselves in Jesus' conversation with the lawyer who wants to inherit eternal life. When prompted, the lawyer responds to Jesus by quoting the heart of the Law from the Old Testament: "You shall love the Lord your God with all your heart, and with all your soul, and with all your strength, and with all your mind; and your neighbor as yourself" (Luke 10:25–27).

The story does not end there, however. It is just beginning. The lawyer, "desiring to justify himself, said to Jesus, 'And who is my neighbor?'" (Luke 10:29). Jesus responds with the parable of the Good Samaritan. Before we unpack the parable, let us pause for a moment and consider what does *not* happen. After all, we can sense a bit of aggression in the lawyer's question: "Who is my neighbor?" While the lawyer may genuinely want to know the answer, his tone hints at resistance.

But notice how Jesus does *not* respond. Jesus does not respond with anger, arrogance, or aggression. Instead, by responding with the parable, Jesus seeks to go deeper. In this, we can learn much about how Jesus loves, especially how Jesus loves *us*. Jesus always desires to take us deeper.

Jesus will always meet us where we are in life. He never expects us to be who we are not or where we are not. Jesus loves us as we are, where we are. But Jesus also loves us too much to leave us in a lesser place. While he is forever meeting us on our terms, he is also forever longing to lead us on his terms. There is always more that he wants to give us, more he wants to show us, and more he wants to heal in us. Jesus wants to go deeper.

At the same time, Jesus has perfect reverence for our free will. Jesus respects us too much to force us to go deeper. He longs for depth in his relationship with us, but we have to choose to go deeper with him.

Any healthy relationship has depth. This is true for good friends, dating couples, and husbands and wives. What makes their relationships healthy is that they choose to have substantial conversations, not superficial ones. At some point, each of those relationships eventually includes conversations that are personal, conversations that go deeper.

When we go deeper with God, we get more personal. We tell him not only what we need, but why we need it. We not only pray for others, but we share with God what they mean to us and how we feel about their need for prayer. Depth requires us to be specific and acknowledge the deepest details in our heart.

This week as we unpack the parable of the Good Samaritan, let us give the Lord permission to take us deeper. He is inviting us, but he is also waiting for us to give him permission.

For Your Prayer

Stay here for an additional ten minutes. Today pray with Psalm 139:1–16. Trust the one who is speaking to you through those words and give him permission to take you deeper.

What words stood out to you as you prayed?
What did you find stirring in your heart?

Compassion

"But a Samaritan, as he journeyed, came to where he was; and when he saw him, he had compassion."

—LUKE 10:33

As Jesus tells the parable of the Good Samaritan, he reveals his heart to all who are listening. In his masterpiece *Jesus of Nazareth,* Pope Benedict XVI reminds us that, in a sense, the Good Samaritan is Jesus, and we are the man who has been left for dead. Because of Original Sin, we are like the man in the parable. We have been wounded and left suffering at the side of the road. But just as the Good Samaritan takes the initiative to save the man left for dead, Jesus takes the initiative to come save us.

The parable reveals much, and over the next three days, we will unpack three aspects of it. Today let us focus on Luke 10:33: "But a Samaritan, as he journeyed, came to where he was; and when he saw him, he had compassion." *Compassion.* What is compassion? When Jesus says that the Samaritan saw him with compassion, what is he telling us?

The Latin root for the word "compassion" is *pati,* which means "to suffer," and the prefix *com-,* which means "with." *Compassion,* then, literally means "to suffer with." The Good Samaritan seems unafraid of the mess he finds when he comes upon the man on the road, wounded and suffering and left for dead. He treats the man's wounds, of course—but let us not forget that the Good Samaritan also enters into the man's suffering.

Jesus is love. Love is something you *do.* Love propels Jesus to be with us, always. Jesus is compassion itself, which means Jesus desires to suffer with us. There is nothing in our lives, including our suffering, that is too much for Jesus or that would compel him to leave us. In fact, my personal experience has taught me that the place where I need healing the most is precisely the place where Jesus wants to meet me.

Many of us have our own personal stories of hurt, sin, and struggle. Many of us have brought these things to the light and are free. But some of us may have buried them deep within. Thus, yesterday's invitation to go deeper may elicit fear, for there may be an element of self-protection that causes us to resist going there. We may be afraid to go deeper because we are aware of things that are buried deep within our hearts.

Do not be afraid. Jesus *is* compassion. Jesus, like the Good Samaritan, is longing to enter into our woundedness. It is important for us to remember that Jesus only wants to go deeper so that he can bring healing. There is never condemnation, judgment, or accusation. The Heart of Compassion is not afraid to suffer with us. He longs to bring healing.

Do not be afraid. Jesus *is* love. Jesus *is* compassion.

For Your Prayer

Stay here for an additional ten minutes. Today pray with Luke 10:33. Be present in the scene. Be there with Jesus. Ask the Holy Spirit to help you be in the place of the man in need of healing. Imagine the scene unfolding as it does in the Bible, but imagine that you are there too and that Jesus himself is the Good Samaritan.

What words stood out to you as you prayed?
What did you find stirring in your heart?

_____

_____

_____

_____

_____

_____

_____

_____

_____

_____

_____

_____

_____

_____

_____

_____

_____

_____

_____

_____

_____

Messy

"He had compassion, and went to him and bound up his wounds, pouring on oil and wine."

—LUKE 10:33–34

Today we continue to unpack the parable of the Good Samaritan. Yesterday I mentioned that there are three aspects of the parable worthy of our consideration, the first being the compassion of the Samaritan and the way he enters into the man's suffering. Today let us consider how the Good Samaritan "went to him and bound up his wounds, pouring on oil and wine" (Luke 10:34).

Why is this compelling for us to consider? Jesus says that the robbers left the man "half dead" (Luke 10:30). Consider what that meant. The man had been robbed. He had been assaulted. He had been beaten *badly*, almost fatally. We shudder to imagine the blood, the grotesque condition of his flesh, and the filth he was left to lie in. These details, while graphic and distressing to imagine, are important to bear in mind. Why? Because they show us precisely the reality into which the Good Samaritan enters.

Jesus said that the Good Samaritan bound up the man's wounds and poured oil and wine on them. You cannot do such a thing from afar; you can only do it up close. The Good Samaritan would have seen the mess, touched it, and smelled it. The Good Samaritan would have had to get messy himself. In the binding and caring and pouring, the Good Samaritan could not stand at a distance. He chose instead to enter the mess and get messy himself.

Whew! Ponder that. This is precisely the image of himself that Jesus wants to portray. Jesus is not afraid to enter our mess. Jesus is not afraid to get messy. Because he *is* compassion, he is not afraid to suffer with us. He is not afraid to go deeper into our mess and get messy with us.

Imagine how this idea would have affected those listening to Jesus. There would have been hundreds, maybe thousands of people following Jesus day after day. While Luke does not tell us exactly how many were listening, we certainly can deduce who was listening. Jesus certainly attracted people like his twelve Apostles and the seventy-two disciples. But he also attracted sinners and outcasts. Ancient Judaism had rules and labels for those who were considered "clean" or "unclean," holy or not. People on the fringes of society, especially those who had sin and shame as a part of their story, would have been all too familiar with the consequences of their messy history. Imagine what is in their hearts as they hear Jesus tell them that he, the Messiah, is not afraid of their mess.

A person has to be intimately close to pour oil and wine in another's wounds and bind them up. Here's the good news: Jesus wants to get that close to *you*. Jesus wants to heal you, just as the Good Samaritan healed the man left for dead. Jesus is not afraid of your mess. Jesus is not afraid to get messy.

For Your Prayer

Stay here for an additional ten minutes. Today pray with Luke 10:34. Be present in the scene. Be there with Jesus. Ask the Holy Spirit to help you be in the place of the man in need of healing. Imagine the scene unfolding as it does in the Bible, but imagine that you are there too and that Jesus himself is the Good Samaritan.

What words stood out to you as you prayed?
What did you find stirring in your heart?

Lavish

"Then he set him on his own beast and brought him to an inn, and took care of him. And the next day he took out two denarii and gave them to the innkeeper, saying, 'Take care of him; and whatever more you spend, I will repay you when I come back.'"

—LUKE 10:34–35

On Monday I mentioned there were three aspects of the parable of the Good Samaritan that are worthy of our consideration. We have discussed the first two aspects, the first being the compassion of the Good Samaritan and the second being his willingness to get close to the man and enter into his mess. Today let us consider the third aspect, that the Good Samaritan "set him on his own beast and brought him to an inn, and took care of him. And the next day he took out two denarii and gave them to the innkeeper, saying, 'Take care of him; and whatever more you spend, I will repay you when I come back'" (Luke 10:34–35).

It would have been enough for the Good Samaritan to stop and check on the man left for dead, but he did more. It would have been enough for the Good Samaritan to pour oil and wine on the man's wounds and bandage them, but he did *more*. Jesus tells us that the Good Samaritan not only bent over backward to give the man immediate care and attention, but he also went out of his way to bring the man to the shelter and comfort of an inn and paid the innkeeper to take care of him.

Let us dwell a moment with an often-overlooked part of the story. The Good Samaritan says, "Take care of him; and whatever more you spend, I will repay you when I come back." Notice that there is no budget. There is no limit. Whatever the innkeeper spends in caring for the man, the Good Samaritan will repay himself. Jesus pushes the limits of our imagination with this lavish generosity.

Jesus' love is lavish beyond anything else; it is without limit. Jesus' desire to heal us is lavish, without limit. Jesus' compassion, desire, and initiative are lavish, without limit.

Many of us have been shaped by the conditional way we love and the conditional way we are loved. Few of us know people who are unafraid of our mess, and even fewer of us have encountered truly unconditional love. There can be a quiet temptation lurking deep within that tries to convince us, "Your mess is too much. People will be repelled by or grow tired of your woundedness." Some of us may have experienced "letting people into" our hearts. But it takes a lot to truly be with others in their mess. Many of us may know too well our own limitations and the limits others have in loving us.

Here's the good news: Jesus is lavish. His love knows *no* limits. Jesus has more than enough love for you. Your wounds and your mess are not too much for him. Jesus is pure love, and his love is lavish.

For Your Prayer

Stay here for an additional ten minutes. Today pray with Luke 10:34–35. Be present in the scene. Be there with Jesus. Ask the Holy Spirit to help you be in the place of the man in need of healing. Imagine the scene unfolding as it does in the Bible, but imagine that you are there too. Imagine that Jesus himself is the Good Samaritan. What specific wounds in your heart do you need Jesus to heal?

What words stood out to you as you prayed?
What did you find stirring in your heart?

_____

_____

_____

_____

_____

_____

_____

_____

_____

_____

_____

_____

_____

_____

_____

_____

_____

_____

_____

_____

_____

_____

_____

_____

Relate

"Lord, do you not care that my sister has left me to serve alone? Tell her then to help me."

—LUKE 10:40

As we continue the journey to Jerusalem, we next read that "as they went on their way, [Jesus] entered a village; and a woman named Martha received him into her house" (Luke 10:38). What follows, of course, is the story of Martha and Mary. This story is probably familiar to you. Jesus visits the sisters in their home. As Mary sits at his feet, listening to him, Martha struggles to get food on the table. Upset with her sister for not lending a hand, she asks Jesus to tell Mary to help her. Instead, Jesus tells her that Mary has chosen "the good portion, which shall not be taken away from her" (Luke 10:42).

I have been a priest for more than twenty years. I have read this story hundreds of times. I have preached about this text on more occasions than I can remember. I have heard others comment on the story. Far too often, the emphasis is on Mary, with a judgment toward Martha. But I'd like to take you a little deeper this time so you can appreciate Martha's integrity.

Martha is rightly corrected by the Lord—but notice that she is aware of her emotions and honest enough to share them with Jesus in the moment. She does not try to be who she is not. She does not pretend or deflect. Martha has a lot in her heart, and she relates it all to Jesus. Her words are "Lord, do you not care that my sister has left me to serve alone? Tell her then to help me" (Luke 10:40). Her feelings are raw. They are real. And Martha does not ruminate on them; she does not keep them circling in her own head. She tells Jesus exactly what she is feeling.

What is in our hearts matters less than what we do with what is in our hearts. The important thing is that nothing is off-limits with Jesus. As we go deeper with Jesus, it is important to give him permission to go there with us—and to give ourselves permission to be honest with the Lord. There is a difference between thinking about Jesus and actually talking with Jesus. There is a difference between thinking about our mess and talking with Jesus honestly about our mess. When we are stuck on the treadmill of rumination, we always leave exhausted. But when we have the courage to share the deepest movements of our hearts with the Lord, we always put ourselves in a position to be known and loved.

Martha, in my humble opinion, is an example of someone who has the courage to be honest with Jesus. Of course, she is rightly corrected by the Lord. But even his gentle correction would not have been possible had she not been honest with him to begin with.

Regardless of what pops up when you go deeper, do not be afraid. Relate everything to Jesus. Share every emotion, every thought, every fear, every desire, every question. Share everything. Relate everything to the Lord.

For Your Prayer

Stay here for an additional ten minutes. Today pray with Luke 10:38–42. Be present in the scene. Be there with Jesus. Ask the Holy Spirit to help you experience the home of Martha and Mary. Imagine the scene unfolding as it does in the Bible, but imagine that you are there too, that Jesus is seeking to listen to everything in your heart.

What words stood out to you as you prayed?
What did you find stirring in your heart?

Not

"And ought not this woman, a
daughter of Abraham whom Satan
bound for eighteen years,
be loosed from this bond
on the sabbath day?"

—LUKE 13:16

A little later in Luke's account of the journey to Jerusalem, we read that Jesus "was teaching in one of the synagogues on the sabbath" (Luke 13:10). What follows is the story of Jesus healing a crippled woman. Luke tells us, "There was a woman who had had a spirit of infirmity for eighteen years; she was bent over and could not fully straighten herself. And when Jesus saw her, he called her and said to her, 'Woman, you are freed from your infirmity.' And he laid his hands upon her, and immediately she was made straight, and she praised God" (Luke 13:11–13).

What happens next is unexpected. Most people would greet such an outpouring of mercy and healing with awe and wonder. But this healing provokes anger. Luke writes that "the ruler of the synagogue, indignant because Jesus had healed on the sabbath, said to the people, 'There are six days on which work ought to be done; come on those days and be healed, and not on the sabbath day.' Then the Lord answered him, 'You hypocrites! Does not each of you on the sabbath untie his ox or his donkey from the manger, and lead it away to water it? And ought not this woman, a daughter of Abraham whom Satan bound for eighteen years, be loosed from this bond on the sabbath day?'" (Luke 13:14–16)

Jesus' love is so fierce that he refuses to be bound by anyone or anything. Jesus' love brings hope and healing. Jesus' love is mercy and compassion. However, Jesus' love again seems to be too much for some people. They are shocked by the limitless nature of his lavish love. We read that the ruler of the synagogue becomes "indignant." The word *indignant* implies arrogance and a sense of self-righteousness. The ruler of the synagogue is blind to what Jesus is doing because Jesus is not doing it the way the establishment was expecting. But Jesus is not bound by their boxes, categories, and labels.

If we press further into the scene, we also notice the fierce nature of Jesus' impassioned heart. Jesus calls out the hypocrisy of those who are blind to him. Doing so sends a signal to those in leadership but also to those on the fringe, those who have been judged by the religious authorities. Jesus will *not* be bound by anyone or anything. Jesus will *not* be stopped by those who are afraid. He will *not* be prevented from accomplishing the end for which he came: to restore all humanity to communion with God.

Nothing will stop him. He will *not* be stopped.

For Your Prayer

Stay here for an additional ten minutes. Today pray with Luke 13:10–17. Be present in the scene. Be there with Jesus. Ask the Holy Spirit to help you experience the synagogue. Imagine the scene unfolding as it does in the Bible, but imagine that you are there too. Be with Jesus and feel the intensity of his love.

What words stood out to you as you prayed?
What did you find stirring in your heart?

_____

_____

_____

_____

_____

_____

_____

_____

_____

_____

_____

_____

_____

_____

_____

_____

_____

_____

_____

_____

_____

_____

_____

Where

"*He went on his way through towns and villages, teaching, and journeying toward Jerusalem.*"

—LUKE 13:22

Saturday of the
Second Week of Lent

L et us return to something we pondered on Tuesday—namely, what was in the hearts and minds of those who encountered Jesus on his journey. This week we have experienced many things on the road to Jerusalem: the parable of the Good Samaritan, the experience of Martha and Mary, and the healing of a woman on the Sabbath. These things would have affected people in different ways.

Let us imagine what was in the hearts of those closest to Jesus: his mother, the twelve Apostles, and the women who helped provide for them. Then there were the seventy-two disciples, along with the scribes and Pharisees. And on the outskirts of the crowds, there were the sinners and the outcasts. Let us imagine all of them today.

As we wrap up this second week of Lent, I would like to lead you in a guided meditation. Let us begin by asking the Holy Spirit to awaken our spiritual senses as we pray. May we receive the gift to see what those in the Gospel saw, to hear what they heard, and to feel what they felt.

Imagine that we are all walking on a long, hot road. With the Sea of Galilee behind us and the desert in front of us, we are in the massive crowd that follows Jesus on this journey to Jerusalem. Imagine what is in the hearts of the Apostles as they witness Jesus loving with such unbridled mercy and limitless love. Certainly, they are also looking deep within their own hearts. While much of their day is taken up with crowd control, monitoring the mass of people surrounding Jesus, they are also experiencing their own ongoing conversions. They are deeply affected by Jesus' message and powerful presence.

Then there are the scribes and Pharisees. They too are on this journey. They too are witnessing Jesus' miracles with their own eyes, but they do not know what to do with this Jesus who operates outside of their boxes and their categories.

Finally, if you listen carefully, you can hear the sacred tears of sinners who have been moved by Jesus' mercy and compassion. Never before have the people on the fringes met someone like Jesus. For the first time ever, many of them are feeling hope and the desire to give their lives to God. Their tears are a sign that God is truly with them in their suffering.

And then there is you. You too are on this journey to Jerusalem. You too are watching all these things unfold before your eyes. The question for you at the end of this second week of Lent is this: Where do you find yourself walking on the journey? Are you drawn to walk with the Apostles and those who are experiencing ongoing conversion? Or do you resonate more with the sinners and those on the fringe? Do you desire to walk up front, right at Jesus' side? Or are you somewhere in between, not knowing exactly where you fit in?

For Your Prayer

Stay here for an additional ten minutes. Reread the guided meditation above, and then close your eyes and imagine yourself in the scene. Do not read along with the book, but instead ask the Holy Spirit to let you see what the people in the scene saw, hear what they heard, and feel what they felt. Allow his inspiration, and journal about the fruit that comes from your prayer.

What words stood out to you as you prayed?
What did you find stirring in your heart?

_____

_____

_____

_____

_____

_____

_____

_____

_____

_____

_____

_____

_____

_____

_____

_____

_____

_____

_____

_____

_____

Here are three questions to help you reflect on this week's meditations. You may find it helpful to discuss them with others or ponder them on your own before you begin the weekly reflection:

- Have you experienced Jesus' limitless compassion? In what ways has Jesus entered into your suffering? What wounds are you asking him to heal for you?

- As we explored this week (and will continue to explore in future weeks), Jesus made certain religious authorities uncomfortable because he did not fit into their preconceived "boxes" and he challenged their understanding of the Law. In what ways have you put Jesus into a box of your own? What self-imposed limits have you placed on his love and mercy? Do you believe he is willing to love you in your mess? How is Jesus calling you to a deeper understanding of who he is and the healing he wants to bring to your life?

- **VIDEO REFLECTION:** Take a moment to study the painting of the Good Samaritan that Fr. Toups mentions, painted by Johan Carl Loth. (You might also look up other "Good Samaritan" paintings by other artists, e.g., Rembrandt or Van Gogh.) As you look at the artwork(s), imagine yourself in the position of the wounded man and Jesus as the Good Samaritan. What would you say to Jesus as he comes to you in the place where you need to be loved the most?

Now take a moment to reflect on the past week, going over the meditations that bore the most fruit in your prayer, the things you wrote, and your reflections on this week's video. How has your prayer changed this week?

Listen

Which

"And the Pharisees and the scribes murmured, saying, 'This man receives sinners and eats with them.'"

—LUKE 15:2

A s we begin this third week of Lent, I would like to lead you
in another guided meditation. Let us begin today by asking
the Holy Spirit to awaken our spiritual senses as we pray. May
we receive the gift to see what those in the Gospel saw, to hear
what they heard, and to feel what they felt.

Imagine that Jesus' journey to Jerusalem has brought him to
a tall hilltop. As you enter the scene, you can feel a particular
intentionality in his presence. He seems poised to teach today,
and you can sense that the message that will soon pour forth from
his lips has been anchored in his heart for quite some time. As he
beholds the massive crowd that has gathered for today's teaching,
he sees much more than their outward appearance. Jesus sees
their longings and needs. He knows their mistakes and pain. He
stands in the midst of their sin and suffering.

Immediately around Jesus sit the twelve Apostles. What is
happening within their hearts? On the one hand, they feel honored
to be a part of Jesus' inner circle. On the other hand, they are still
in the early stages of their own conversions. They long to follow
Jesus with complete dedication, but they are still dealing with their
own ingrained patterns of self-sufficiency and self-centeredness.

Surrounding the Apostles are the scribes and Pharisees. They
know a lot about God and can recite all the right texts about his
love. But many of them are unable to experience the Lord's love
in their own heart. Their constant theological inquisition is a
subtle form of resistance to Jesus' message of mercy.

Surrounding them are the seventy-two disciples. These men
and women have a great desire to know Jesus better and learn
from him. They have not yet chosen to abandon their former

way of life, but they have an authentic desire to go deeper with the Master. They often wish that they were able to be as close to Jesus as the Apostles are.

In the outer circle are the tax collectors and sinners who also want to listen to Jesus. They have heard of him. Some are here because they are curious to see what "the new guy" is preaching. Others are there because they heard Jesus tell the story of the Good Samaritan. The outcasts on the outer fringe are innately intrigued with the purity of love and mercy that radiates from Jesus' heart and words.

Thousands have gathered to hear Jesus. Everyone is here because they want to listen to what Jesus has to say. And you are here too.

Yesterday you had the opportunity to think about which group of people you find yourself drawn to on this journey. Reflect once more on that group today. Which circle feels most comfortable to you? As you place yourself in the scene, which group do you identify with the most? And, most importantly, why do you identify with that group? What is in your heart as you are sitting here with the others? What do you long to hear Jesus say to you?

For Your Prayer

Stay here for an additional ten minutes. Today pray with Luke 15. Read the whole chapter. Then reread the meditation above. Close your eyes and imagine yourself in the scene. Do not read along with the book but instead ask the Holy Spirit to let you see what the people in the scene saw, hear what they heard, and feel what they felt. Allow his inspiration, and journal about the fruit that comes from your prayer.

What words stood out to you as you prayed?
What did you find stirring in your heart?

Listen

"Rejoice with me, for I have found my sheep which was lost."

—LUKE 15:6

Yesterday we painted the scene describing the various groups that have gathered to listen to Jesus. Jesus' presence has filled people with such a tangible sense of hope that even "the tax collectors and sinners were all drawing near to hear him" (Luke 15:1). Those on the outskirts of the crowd are the hungriest, the ones who need God's mercy the most. Jesus is aware that they have often searched for happiness in the wrong places. Thus, as he begins to teach about mercy, Jesus begins with the parable of the lost sheep.

Like the Good Shepherd who seeks his lost sheep, Jesus paints an invitation to repentance on the canvas of this parable. It is especially for the sinners "drawing near to hear him." It is the story of the shepherd who searches for the lost sheep "until he finds it"—and, when he has found it, "lays it on his shoulders, rejoicing" (Luke 15:4–5).

But why on his shoulders? In John 10:27, we read, "My sheep hear my voice, and I know them, and they follow me." However, sheep often go astray, just as we do. So, from the beginning of its life, the shepherd sets a baby lamb on his shoulders so that the lamb comes to know his voice. The shepherd holds the lamb, day in and day out—and once returned to the flock, the lamb never strays again. The voice of the shepherd has become intimately familiar, so the lamb will follow it.

Sheep will stray if they listen to the wrong voice. In the same way, Jesus—the Good Shepherd—knows that sinners stray because we listen to the wrong voice.

Imagine what stirs in the hearts of those on the outer circles as they listen to Jesus describing a God who goes in search of the lost sheep. How many in that outer circle have felt lost themselves? How many have feared their sins are so great that even God has given up on them? Imagine how they feel as they listen to Jesus.

There is a cacophony of voices within each of us. Sometimes we listen to a voice of temptation. Sometimes we listen to a voice of accusation after we have sinned. Sometimes we listen to a voice of discouragement as we attempt to go back to God. We listen to these voices far too often.

If we listen to the voice of Jesus, we will *always* hear a message of mercy. When we listen to Jesus, we hear the voice of the Good Samaritan, who longs to enter our lives. We hear the voice of the Savior, who is pleased to embrace our mess. We hear the voice of the Good Shepherd, who tirelessly calls us to an encounter. The more we learn to listen to Jesus, the more our lives will be anchored in mercy.

For Your Prayer

Stay here for an additional ten minutes. Today pray with Luke 15:1–7. Be there. Be present in the scene. Be with Jesus in the crowd. Listen as Jesus speaks tenderly of the lost sheep. Pay attention to what stirs within you.

What words stood out to you as you prayed?
What did you find stirring in your heart?

_____

_____

_____

_____

_____

_____

_____

_____

_____

_____

_____

_____

_____

_____

_____

_____

_____

_____

_____

_____

_____

_____

_____

_____

_____

Restless

"The younger son collected all his belongings and set off to a distant country."

—LUKE 15:13 NAB

L uke 15 certainly speaks of the mercy of God. After the parable of the lost sheep, Jesus tells the parable of the lost coin—again, a story of someone who loses something precious and searches without giving up until she finds it. These stories would have meant much to those listening to Jesus' words, especially those in the outer circle. But as powerful as those parables are, imagine how much more would have stirred in the hearts of those who listened to the parable of the Prodigal Son.

The first part of the parable of the Prodigal Son describes the wayward wandering of a younger son who takes his inheritance and leaves the security of his home to "set off to a distant country" (Luke 15:13 NAB). As Jesus speaks of the young man's wanderings, you can imagine his eyes locked on the sinners, who feel as if Jesus is reading their souls. As I imagine myself in the crowd that day, a question forms as I listen to Jesus: "Why did the younger son leave?"

Later in this story, the father says to the older son, "Son, you are always with me, and all that is mine is yours" (Luke 15:31). Certainly, the generosity of this father would have been offered equally to both sons. As Jesus describes the father's heart, we imagine that both sons knew that everything that belonged to the father was theirs. So if the younger son lived with a father who wanted to share *everything* with him, why did he leave? What was so intriguing about life on the outside that it caused the younger son to leave a father who says "all that is mine is yours"?

Let us imagine that those on the outskirts of the crowd are asking the same question: "Why did he leave the father?" In reality, the sinners in the outermost circles probably identify with the younger son. Reflecting on their own lives as they listen to Jesus, perhaps they also ask themselves, "Why did I leave the Father?"

The younger son—who is, in a sense, all of us—leaves because he is restless. For some of us, when things get too quiet in our lives, when we can't hear the voice of God, we listen to the voices within: the voices of temptation, accusation, and discouragement that we mentioned yesterday. But there is also a voice of fear that speaks in the silence. Some of us are afraid of loneliness. Some of us are afraid of failure. Some of us are afraid that we're not good enough.

Whatever our fear is, when things get too quiet, we often listen to the voice of fear, and we get restless. If we have the courage to look at our lives, perhaps we'll notice that what leads us into sin is restlessness within.

Take courage and trust the process. Spend some time today with Jesus and ask yourself: "Am I restless? When do I get restless? How do I act when I get restless?"

For Your Prayer

Stay here for an additional ten minutes. Today pray with Luke 15:11–19. Be with Jesus as he looks at the tax collectors and sinners and speaks to them. How do they respond to Jesus? What stirs in your heart as Jesus speaks of the restless son who leaves? Why did the son leave his father? Why do you leave the Father?

What words stood out to you as you prayed?
What did you find stirring in your heart?

Rest

"While he was still a long way off, his father caught sight of him, and was filled with compassion."

—LUKE 15:20 NAB

Our restlessness will eventually catch up with us. St. Augustine writes that "our heart is restless, until it rest in Thee."[11] We are restless when we always need something more in order to accept ourselves: more money for security, more success for self-worth, more acceptance from others. Whatever the voice of restlessness sounds like in our lives, most of us will eventually hear an echo of the question, "Is this what life is really about? Why do I keep doing _____?"

In the parable of the Prodigal Son, the younger son lives a wild life after leaving home and eventually finds himself down and out among strangers. He is hungry and miserable and far from home. We can assume that he finally finds himself tired of being tired, "so he got up and went back to his father" (Luke 15:20 NAB).

Imagine what is going through the son's mind as he travels back home. He wonders if he will be punished by his father and rejected by his family. He imagines shame will follow him forever. Yesterday and the day before we talked about the voices that whisper to us in silence. We can only imagine what whispers torment the younger son as he gets closer to home.

As the parable continues, we read, "While he was still a long way off, his father caught sight of him, and was filled with compassion" (Luke 15:20 NAB). As we listen to Jesus deliver the parable, we can imagine the father going out every day to look out for his son. Yes—it is the father who is looking, not the son! It is the father who "caught sight of him," whose eyes are "filled with compassion."

Imagine what it must have been like for the son when his father embraced him. This restless son who abandoned his father is now held close, even in his sin. The compassion that radiates from the heart of the father pierces the fears of the son. The son's former restlessness is drowned in mercy—and finally, he can rest in the truth of his father's love.

Most of our restlessness is driven by the lies we listen to. We may be restless because we don't like something deep within us. Then we become fearful, and soon we seek escape. We become restless because of the deeper things in us that make us afraid.

Yesterday you thought about why the son left his father and why you leave the Father. Today ask Jesus about what causes your restlessness. As you do, remember that Jesus only wants what is best for you. Jesus wants you to rest. Ask the Lord to help you grow in self-awareness as you ask him what within you makes you restless.

For Your Prayer

Stay here for an additional ten minutes. Today pray with Luke 15:11–24. Be with Jesus as he looks at tax collectors and sinners. How do they respond to Jesus? What stirs in your heart as Jesus speaks about the compassion of the Father?

What words stood out to you as you prayed?
What did you find stirring in your heart?

Inadequate

"Father, I have sinned against heaven and before you; I am no longer worthy to be called your son."

—LUKE 15:21

The outermost circle of tax collectors and sinners must have been stunned by this captivating parable of mercy. As Jesus describes the compassionate father who yearns for his son's return, the crowd's silence is piercing. Imagine how powerfully Jesus' teaching affects those on the fringes of society.

As I explained earlier, ancient Judaism was filled with codes and classes, myriad classifications detailing what was permitted and not permitted, who was clean and unclean. Thousands fall outside the "good" categories, yet they all yearn for God's love. As Jesus teaches about the son's situation and the father's compassion, their hearts are moved and their eyes fill with tears. The sinners feel as if they are in the story. This parable is no longer about a fictitious son; this is about them.

Jesus continues the parable with the son's quick response to his father's gratuitous mercy. The son, ashamed, admits, "Father, I have sinned against heaven and before you; I am no longer worthy to be called your son" (Luke 15:21). The son is shackled by his shame and feels inadequate.

The father, however, is filled with mercy and love. Loving his son despite the son's judgment of himself, the father orders his servants to start the feast because, as he says, "my son was dead, and is alive again; he was lost, and is found" (Luke 15:24). The son is consumed with shame, seeing only his mistakes; the father, on the other hand, sees the son as a father sees his child: his flesh, his beloved.

One of our deepest fears is that we are inadequate. Many of us quietly fear deep within that if people really knew us, they would not love us. This fear of who we think we are, this fear of inadequacy, drives many people to try to prove themselves professionally or financially. It may drive others to an inordinate obsession with their body or with looking a certain age. Because of the way we see ourselves, we may find ourselves always trying to prove ourselves.

Jesus doesn't look at us through our eyes; he looks at us through his eyes. Jesus' eyes are the eyes of love. He sees us, and he sees our inadequacies. But he sees us as our *selves*: he doesn't see us as our inadequacies.

Where you feel inadequate is where you feel most restless. Jesus wants you to rest. Ask Jesus what he sees when he sees you.

For Your Prayer

Stay here for an additional ten minutes. Today pray with Luke 15:20–24. Be with Jesus as he looks at tax collectors and sinners. How do they respond to Jesus? What stirs in your heart as Jesus speaks of the Father? Where do you feel inadequate? How does Jesus feel about your inadequacy?

What words stood out to you as you prayed?
What did you find stirring in your heart?

_____

_____

_____

_____

_____

_____

_____

_____

_____

_____

_____

_____

_____

_____

_____

_____

_____

_____

_____

_____

_____

_____

_____

Found

"He was lost, and is found."

—LUKE 15:24

Imagine the silence of the crowd. They are all speechless: the prostitutes, the thieves, the lepers. All those judged by society and judged by themselves listen, speechless, stunned by Jesus' piercing love and mercy. The parable of the Prodigal Son comes to its triumphant climax as the father exclaims, "My son was dead, and is alive again; he was lost, and is found" (Luke 15:24).

The son was lost. He was restless. He was shackled in shame and fear. Yet he has been found. There is no judgment from the father. There is no anger. There is no scorecard. There is only mercy and love. The father rejoices that he has found his son.

There have been many times in my own life when I have felt lost. At such times, I feel trapped, as if there is no way out. Whenever I feel lost, I feel as if there is no solution. I feel hopeless. I grow afraid.

I wonder if you have ever felt this way.

There are temptations I face when I feel lost. I am tempted to believe that no one is looking for me. I am tempted to believe that it is my own fault that I am lost. Then I am tempted to believe there is something wrong with me, which led me into the mess I am in. Thus, I am tempted to believe that others have grown tired of my brokenness and have given up on me. These thoughts whisper to me that no one is coming to find me. In a cycle of self-accusation, I grow more and more restless—and this restlessness leads to self-sufficiency, where I try to control everything myself. Instead of trusting that someone is looking for me and will find me, I try to manage my life on my own.

When you feel lost, don't panic. In those moments when your thoughts and emotions seek to deceive you, I encourage you to use your intellect. *Remember.* Remember what Jesus said about himself and what he has revealed to us about God. Jesus is *always* looking for you. So, put yourself in a position to be found. Ask him to find you. Trust that he will find you.

You really can stop running. You don't have to earn your way back to Jesus. You don't have to manage life all on your own. Try to be relentlessly honest with yourself and do everything you can to surrender your life and your situation to God. Then, trust that God is tirelessly calling you, looking at you through his eyes and loving you like the father of the Prodigal Son.

For Your Prayer

Stay here for an additional ten minutes. Today pray with Luke 15:11–24. Be with Jesus. What stirs in your heart as you hear the father rejoice that his son has been found? Is there any place in your own life where you feel lost? Is there any place in your own life where you need to be found?

What words stood out to you as you prayed?
What did you find stirring in your heart?

_____

_____

_____

_____

_____

_____

_____

_____

_____

_____

_____

_____

_____

_____

_____

_____

_____

_____

_____

_____

_____

_____

Alone

"In these days he went out to the hills to pray; and all night he continued in prayer to God."

—LUKE 6:12

Saturday of the
Third Week of Lent

As we end this third week of Lent with a guided meditation, let us ask the Holy Spirit to inspire us as we pray. Let us ask the Holy Spirit to awaken our spiritual senses. May we receive the gift to see what those in the Gospel saw, to hear what they heard, and to feel what they felt.

Imagine that Jesus has finished delivering this splendid teaching on the mercy of God. The crowd is silent. The hearts of the people are full. One by one the groups disband, and the people leave.

The Apostles are instructed to move on and prepare the way to the next village where Jesus will soon teach. The scribes and Pharisees have also left the scene. They too have been moved by Jesus' compassion, but they don't know what to do with it. They don't know what to do with this teacher who radiates such love. The seventy-two disciples go off to think about the teaching, and they begin to talk among themselves about their own wayward pasts.

The circle of sinners is the last to depart. Mercy has been poured into their hearts today. Some are weeping. Others are simply stunned in silence. After focusing so much of their efforts on perfectly adhering to rules and regulations, the people had forgotten that God loves them even if they aren't perfect. God loves them in the midst of their messiness and imperfections.

Now imagine that they too have departed, and the only people left are you and Jesus. It is just the two of you. You are now alone with Jesus.

Jesus looks at you, and his eyes invite you to join him in private conversation. Feeling both intrigued and afraid, you make your way to the Lord, and he invites you to sit down next to him.

Jesus looks you in the eyes and begins to speak to you. He stuns you with his knowledge of the times in your life when you felt lost. One by one, moment by moment, season by season, with great tenderness and mercy, Jesus tells you the story of your life. You are alone with Jesus, and you feel more deeply known in this moment than ever before.

Jesus then looks at you and says, "In all those moments, you were never alone." Stop to take that in. He says again to you, "You have never been alone." Then, one by one, moment by moment, season by season, Jesus shows you where he was during each of the times you felt lost and alone. Jesus begins to reveal to you how, in each of these moments, *he was with you and longing for you to know him.*

You are alone with Jesus now, and you realize that you have never been alone in your life.

What is in your heart as you are with Jesus? What is he saying particularly to you? What do you want to say in return?

For Your Prayer

Stay here for an additional ten minutes. Reread the guided meditation above, and then close your eyes to imagine yourself in the scene. Do not read along with the book, but instead allow the Holy Spirit to let you see what the people there saw, hear what they heard, and feel what they felt. Allow his inspiration, and journal about the fruit that comes from your prayer.

What words stood out to you as you prayed?
What did you find stirring in your heart?

_____

_____

_____

_____

_____

_____

_____

_____

_____

_____

_____

_____

_____

_____

_____

_____

_____

_____

_____

_____

_____

Here are three questions to help you reflect on this week's meditations. You may find it helpful to discuss them with others or ponder them on your own before you begin the weekly reflection:

- In what ways have you experienced hearing the voice of the Good Shepherd in your life? What can help you better listen to God's voice?

- What aspects of your life make you feel restless right now? What lies have the voices of the world been telling you to tempt you to go astray? Like the loving father in the parable of the Prodigal Son, how is Jesus inviting you to return to him, trust in him, and go deeper with him?

- **VIDEO REFLECTION:** As Fr. Toups says in this video, "Mercy is love bestowed when we don't deserve it." With that thought in mind, what strikes you the most about this painting of *The Return of the Prodigal Son* by Pompeo Batoni?

Now take a moment to reflect on the past week, going over the meditations that bore the most fruit in your prayer, the things you wrote, and your reflections on this week's video. How has your prayer changed this week?

Commit

See

"And at his gate lay a poor man
named Lazarus, full of sores,
who desired to be fed with what fell
from the rich man's table;
moreover the dogs came
and licked his sores."

—LUKE 16:20–21

Jesus is not crucified because everyone loves him. The Gospels tell of Jesus' freedom to lay down his life of his own free will, of course. But there are those who want him dead. They are threatened by his presence, his words, and his identity as the Son of God.

Jesus' love knows no limits. His passion for mercy and his relentless pursuit of those in need eventually pushes the Pharisees too far. It's one thing to love; it is another thing altogether to love as Jesus loves. As we enter the fourth week of Lent, let us be ready for Jesus to push the boundaries.

On the one hand, Jesus' message of mercy liberates the hearts of those bound by shame. On the other hand, Jesus' message of mercy is too much for some of the Pharisees, and tension is building.

Immediately after the parable of the Prodigal Son, Jesus tells the parable of the dishonest steward, a story with implicit reference to the Pharisees. He then condemns their materialism through the parable of the rich man and Lazarus (Luke 16:19–31).

Lazarus was a poor man who begged at the gate of a rich man's house. But the rich man ignored him. When Lazarus died, he went to Father Abraham in heaven. The rich man died and went to hell. The rich man asked Father Abraham to send Lazarus to him with water to cool his anguish, but Father Abraham said no. Then the rich man asked Father Abraham to send Lazarus to his brothers to warn them. But it was too late for that too.

What is striking in this particular parable is the affliction of Lazarus. He is poor. He lives hungry. He is humiliated day after day as he is forced to beg. To highlight Lazarus' suffering, Jesus says,

"Moreover the dogs came and licked his sores" (Luke 16:21). On the heels of the parables of the Good Samaritan and the Prodigal Son, Jesus yet again uses a parable to drive home the fact that he is not afraid of our mess.

What is also striking in this parable is how the rich man is described as having grown so indifferent to Lazarus' suffering that he no longer sees or notices him. Imagine how this detail stirs the hearts of Jesus' listeners. Certainly, the story has stung the conscience of the Pharisees, but think of how it moves the hearts of those who are on the fringes, who are all too familiar with what it is like to be unseen and unnoticed. They hang on Jesus' every word.

When we suffer, we are often tempted to believe that we are alone, that even God has abandoned us. We are tempted to believe that no one sees our hearts. When we suffer, we may be tempted to think that those around us have grown indifferent to our suffering and no longer see us. Jesus' parable drives home the fact that he *sees* Lazarus. He sees suffering. He sees everyone—including you in your suffering.

For Your Prayer

Stay here for an additional ten minutes. Today pray with Luke 16:19–31. Be with Jesus. Listen to him. What stirs in your heart as he teaches the parable?

What words stood out to you as you prayed?
What did you find stirring in your heart?

Distance

"Ten lepers, who stood at a distance ... "

—LUKE 17:12

Monday of the
Fourth Week of Lent

Yesterday we heard Jesus tell the parable of the rich man and Lazarus. Today, "on the way to Jerusalem he was passing along between Samaria and Galilee. And as he entered a village, he was met by ten lepers" (Luke 17:11–12). What is most interesting about this event is four seemingly inconsequential words: that the lepers "stood at a distance" (Luke 17:12).

Distance. They stand at a distance. They are lepers, and according to the Law of Moses, they are required to keep their distance. In first-century Judaism, when a person discovered a skin disorder, he or she had to go to the priest for examination. The priest then determined whether the disease was contagious and if the person was to be declared ceremonially unclean (Leviticus 13:1–46). Jewish law prohibited anyone with such a disease from associating with the general community. They had to be isolated, and many times lived as outcasts until they died (Leviticus 13:45–46). This was necessary to keep infectious diseases from becoming an epidemic. But for those afflicted, it could be a life sentence. It meant a life of distance.

Jesus' response is one of love and mercy: "When he saw them he said to them, 'Go and show yourselves to the priests.' *And as they went* they were cleansed" (Luke 17:14, emphasis added). They are not cleansed immediately; notice that they are cleansed *as they go*. Their leaving to see the priests requires them to believe that Jesus has the power to heal them. (To show up to the priest and not be healed would be humiliating.) They have to believe—and they do. As they go, they are healed.

This all begins when the lepers cry out, "Jesus, Master, have mercy on us" (Luke 17:13). The lepers declare that Jesus is their master.

Their recognition of Jesus' authority even over leprosy is an acknowledgment of him as the Messiah. And if Jesus is the Messiah, that means the distance between us and God is erased. Jesus is God, and the distance is gone.

As we mentioned before, Jesus is "resolutely determined to journey to Jerusalem" (Luke 9:51 NAB) because he has come to erase the distance. In Jesus, God has assumed human flesh so he can be near us, with us, one of us. In Jesus' humanity, all humanity is reclaimed by God; through the self-offering sacrifice of the Paschal Mystery, the distance between humankind and God is erased. All of this will happen in Jerusalem, and that is why you and I are on this journey with Jesus.

How, where, and when in your life does God feel distant? Having the courage to name those particular moments gives him permission to speak to you about his presence there, precisely in the distance you feel. Do not be afraid. Ask him today if he is distant.

For Your Prayer

Stay here for an additional ten minutes. Today pray with Isaiah 43:1–7. Ask the Lord to reveal where he is in your life.

What words stood out to you as you prayed?
What did you find stirring in your heart?

Box

"He also told this parable to some who trusted in themselves that they were righteous and despised others ... "

—LUKE 18:9

Immediately after Jesus heals the lepers, the Pharisees ask him when the kingdom of God will come. The last verses of Luke 17 reveal his answer: it is already in their midst. Then, further in Luke 18, Jesus tells the parable of the Pharisee and the tax collector, a stinging exposure of the Pharisees' hypocrisy.

In Luke 18:10–14, he says, "Two men went up into the temple to pray, one a Pharisee and the other a tax collector. The Pharisee stood and prayed thus with himself, 'God, I thank you that I am not like other men, extortioners, unjust, adulterers, or even like this tax collector. I fast twice a week, I give tithes of all that I get.'" Meanwhile, the tax collector prays simply, "God, be merciful to me a sinner!" To drive home his point, Jesus concludes by explicitly calling out the Pharisees for their arrogance, "for every one who exalts himself will be humbled, but he who humbles himself will be exalted."

In the eyes of the Pharisees, this is getting personal. It is one thing for Jesus to show compassion to sinners; it is another thing altogether for Jesus to explicitly call out the Pharisees. But just as the Pharisees are blind to their own hypocrisy, they are blind to Jesus' true identity, and Jesus is calling them out because of it. The Pharisees are blind because they have put God in a box.

Many people have a box for God. We compartmentalize our lives—"This is my family box. This is my work box. This is my God box." Nice and neat, each aspect of our life is compartmentalized. But Jesus wants everything in our hearts. He wants all of us, including every compartment.

Jesus does not fit in a box. He certainly does not fit in the Pharisees' box for God. Jesus' mercy is passionately unbridled.

His compassion stretches beyond the codes and classifications of first-century Judaism. Yet even with the bold illustrations of mercy and miracles, many people are still blind to the Son of God who stands in the flesh just a few feet in front of them.

During this journey to Jerusalem, not only will hearts be moved to conversion, but tension will build, boil, and then erupt into confrontation. This Jesus whom you have come to know so personally during the first half of Lent is soon to be a hunted man, the object of conspiracy. Why? Because his love and mercy do not fit into a box. Because their pharisaical understanding and expectations of the Messiah do not align with the reality of who Jesus is as the Son of God.

As the tension brews between Jesus and the Pharisees, one can only imagine how it is affecting Jesus' Apostles. Each of them inevitably has his own expectations about who Jesus is and what the future might look like. Things are beginning to grow uncomfortable as Jesus refuses to limit himself to anyone's expectations—even theirs.

For Your Prayer

Stay here for an additional ten minutes. Today pray with Luke 18:10–11. Be present in the scene. Be there with Jesus. Ask the Holy Spirit to help you see what the people in the Gospel saw and hear what they heard. Imagine the scene unfolding as it does in the Bible, but imagine that you are there too. Then, at the end of the scene, imagine that Jesus looks at you. Jesus asks you about your expectations, about the boxes where you often put him. Talk to him about this.

What words stood out to you as you prayed?
What did you find stirring in your heart?

See

"*Behold, we are going up to Jerusalem, and everything that is written of the Son of man by the prophets will be accomplished.*"

—LUKE 18:31

If you thought yesterday's scene was uncomfortable, today's is even more gripping. The journey to Jerusalem continues as Jesus pulls his Apostles aside once again and says to them, "Behold, we are going up to Jerusalem, and everything that is written of the Son of man by the prophets will be accomplished. For he will be delivered to the Gentiles, and will be mocked and shamefully treated and spit upon; they will scourge him and kill him, and on the third day he will rise" (Luke 18:31–33).

The Apostles are absorbing the reality of these words. Jesus says he will be mocked, shamefully treated, and spit upon. Worse, he will be scourged before he is killed.

Killed. He says they will kill him. Oh my—none of this was expected. The Apostles have come to love Jesus. They are his closest followers and friends. They are his most trusted confidants. His prediction of his suffering and death shocks them.

Imagine how this news affects Peter. Jesus changed Peter's life forever. The first time Peter and Jesus met, Peter fell to his knees in humility. Jesus has given him forgiveness, meaning, and purpose. To consider life without Jesus must be painful for Peter.

Imagine how this news affects John. Jesus has also changed John's life forever. Of all the Apostles, John has Jesus' full trust. It is an indication of John's holiness. Their friendship is the fuel for John's holiness. To consider life without Jesus must be painful for John.

Imagine too how this news affects Judas. Judas is with the Twelve when Jesus informs them of his upcoming Passion. We don't know exactly when Judas' heart went off track or how evil first entered it, but hearing Jesus predict his betrayal and death publicly would have been sobering for Judas.

One thing we all experience is life's surprises. Life can sometimes present us with the unexpected. Sometimes a surprise challenges our expectations and sense of control. Sometimes the surprise overwhelms us with fear, grief, or resentment. The thing about surprises is that they often narrow our vision; we can only see what is right in front of us. Jesus, however, can see everything. He sees the present moment when we are surprised, and he sees the future and what he has in store for us.

The key in life is to keep our eyes on the Lord, regardless of the surprises. While we cannot see what God sees, we can trust him. We trust the person, not a viewpoint. We trust in the Lord, who sees much more than we see.

For Your Prayer

Stay here for an additional ten minutes. Today pray with Luke 18:31–34. Be present in the scene. Be there with Jesus. Ask the Holy Spirit to help you see what the people in the Gospel saw and hear what they heard. Imagine the scene unfolding as it does in the Bible, but imagine that you are there too. Then, at the end of the scene, imagine that Jesus looks at you. Jesus asks you how you feel about what he told the Apostles today. How do you respond?

What words stood out to you as you prayed?
What did you find stirring in your heart?

Go

*"As he drew near to Jericho, a blind man
was sitting by the roadside begging ... "*

—LUKE 18:35

A week ago today, we were resting in the lavish mercy of the parable of the Prodigal Son, wrapped in silence as we heard the weeping of sinners on the fringe of society. On the heels of the parable of the Good Samaritan, the parable of the Prodigal Son set a trajectory for this journey to Jerusalem where we all felt bathed in love and mercy.

But how things have changed in the last week. Seven days ago, we were marveling at the mercy of God, and our hearts were resting in hope. Now, a week later, Jesus' overt confrontation with the Pharisees and prediction of his own suffering and death has affected everyone on the journey.

Luke 18 says that Jesus' next stop is Jericho. "As he drew near to Jericho, a blind man was sitting by the roadside begging; and hearing a multitude going by, he inquired what this meant. They told him, 'Jesus of Nazareth is passing by.' And he cried, 'Jesus, Son of David, have mercy on me!' And those who were in front rebuked him, telling him to be silent; but he cried out all the more, 'Son of David, have mercy on me!'" (Luke 18:35–39).

This blind man is described as a beggar. The circumstances of life have forced him to confront his absolute and utter dependence on others. The same is true of his engagement with Jesus. The punctuation in the text is telling: the exclamation points indicate that this man holds nothing back as he begs the Lord for help. Where does he go with his desire? He goes to Jesus.

The story continues: "And Jesus stopped, and commanded him to be brought to him; and when he came near, he asked him, 'What do you want me to do for you?' He said, 'Lord, let me receive my sight.' And Jesus said to him, 'Receive your sight; your faith has made you well.' And immediately he received his sight and followed him, glorifying God; and all the people, when they saw it, gave praise to God" (Luke 18:40–43).

I wonder what is in the hearts of the Apostles as they watch Jesus perform yet another miracle. On the one hand, they must be grateful for the lavish mercy that has changed yet another life. On the other hand, it would be natural for them to ask themselves: If Jesus is powerful enough to heal the blind man, why can't he avoid the impending suffering awaiting him in Jerusalem?

This question is natural for anyone to ask. It is not a matter of whether we have questions for and about God, but instead *where we go* with the questions. We can keep our eyes on the Lord and take our questions and our needs to him, as the blind beggar did—or we can isolate ourselves, ruminate, and fall prey to temptation.

I wonder how and when Judas began to struggle. I often ask myself, "Where did he go with his doubts, his unrest, his questions?" Who knows what would have happened if Judas had gone straight to Jesus? We all know what happened because he did not.

For Your Prayer

Stay here for an additional ten minutes. Today pray with Luke 18:35–43. Be present in the scene. Be there with Jesus. Ask the Holy Spirit to help you see what the people in the Gospel saw and hear what they heard. Imagine the scene unfolding as it does in the Bible, but imagine that you are there too. Pay attention to what stirs within you.

What words stood out to you as you prayed?
What did you find stirring in your heart?

Personal

"He has gone in to be the guest of a man who is a sinner."

—LUKE 19:7

Jesus' journey continues. Luke 19 tells us that Jesus enters Jericho and meets Zacchaeus, whom we know was "a chief tax collector, and rich" (Luke 19:2). Tax collectors were despised by Jews and known to extort even their own kinsmen. They were considered some of the worst sinners imaginable. Therefore, we can only imagine the shock and surprise of the people in the crowd when Jesus "looked up and said to him, 'Zacchaeus, make haste and come down; for I must stay at your house today'" (Luke 19:5).

Jesus continues to push boundaries and climb out of boxes, and not everyone is with him. "And when they saw it they all murmured, 'He has gone in to be the guest of a man who is a sinner'" (Luke 19:7). For a righteous man to enter the house of a tax collector was unimaginable. Jesus' love and mercy is now spilling over into forbidden territory. Many people are outraged.

We have felt a shift this week. On Tuesday Jesus explicitly confronted the Pharisees and essentially called them out for being hypocrites. On Wednesday Jesus looked the Twelve in the eye and predicted his suffering, death, and resurrection. Today Jesus is striding into the home of a tax collector in an overt display of his unbridled desire to seek out the lost. Yes, we have felt a shift this week.

But there is more. In the first week of this journey, we received a new lens through which we see Jesus, that of a Bridegroom coming for his Bride. In the second and third weeks, we unpacked legendary parables of lavish mercy. In the parables of the Good Samaritan and the Prodigal Son, though Jesus was speaking directly to his listeners, he was not speaking about them by name. He was not provoking them directly. Thus, we can appreciate

Jesus' teachings during the first three weeks without discomfort, appreciating the love and mercy with which Jesus speaks and letting it wash over us.

Not this week. This week there has been a shift. The intensity on the journey to Jerusalem is rising. Things are heating up, getting "real" and getting personal. Jesus is calling out the Pharisees in public; it is getting personal for them. We can imagine that Judas is still confined to his self-imposed inner isolation. Judas' inner torment and confusion are compounded by the intensity of the week; it is getting personal for him, too.

And all of it is personal to Jesus. As the Bridegroom who has come to liberate his Bride from sin, Jesus has to confront the very sin and evil that have enslaved humanity. While others are feeling the tension of this week and responding in a variety of ways, the heart of Jesus, the Bridegroom, remains in communion with the Father. The trajectory of this week has only one inevitable outcome; confrontation, conspiracy, and betrayal all await us next week. Jerusalem is mere days away, and much will be happening there.

For Your Prayer

Stay here for an additional ten minutes. Today review the meditations from this week and, if you are journaling, review your journal from this week. Where is your heart at this stage of the journey?

What words stood out to you as you prayed?
What did you find stirring in your heart?

Question

"But he withdrew to the wilderness and prayed."

—LUKE 5:16

Today as we wrap up this fourth week of Lent, I would like to lead you in a guided meditation. Let us begin by asking the Holy Spirit to awaken our spiritual senses as we pray. May we receive the gift to see what those in the Gospel saw, to hear what they heard, and to feel what they felt.

Imagine that you are with Jesus very late in the evening after you and the Apostles entered the home of Zacchaeus for dinner. Before everyone goes to sleep, Jesus invites you, and you alone, to rise early with him in the morning. While Jesus often rises early in the morning to pray, he says nothing more about what you are doing or where you are going. Jesus asked, and you agreed.

Imagine that it is just before sunrise. The sun is still resting beneath the horizon, but the glow of light is slowly casting off the blanket of night. You and Jesus are walking through a grove of olive trees, and with each stride away from the others, you can feel the quiet of solitude drawing the two of you into prayer.

Soon Jesus stops as he eyes a small hill covered with trees but still open to the night sky. The two of you stride up the hill to a place that, as expected, feels secluded but comfortable.

Imagine now that Jesus sits atop a large rock, one that seems perfect for praying. With his right hand, he invites you to sit on the rock to the right of him. Then he looks you in the eye and says, "Thank you for coming. I have longed for time away with the Father, yet it means a lot to me that you are here with me. Sit here with me and let us pray together in silence."

Jesus retreats within to commune with the Father, into a silence where nothing and no one competes for his attention. You can feel the peace radiating from his person as he listens to the Father. The hour passes quickly, as if time has stopped out of reverence for the intimacy of the moment.

Soon Jesus opens his eyes and looks at you. Your eyes lock, as if Jesus is looking through you. You feel known and loved, seen and received. Jesus then says to you, "Our journey to Jerusalem continues. Things are going to get a bit more intense. Some will panic, some will leave, and some will abandon me. But you, promise me that you will stay with me."

Then Jesus asks you: "Will you promise to be there every step of the way? I love you. I called you. I want you there. My mother needs you there. Will you promise to be there?"

For Your Prayer

Stay here for an additional ten minutes. Reread the guided meditation above, and then close your eyes to imagine yourself in the scene. Do not read along with the book, but instead allow the Holy Spirit to let you be present in this special, prayerful moment with Jesus. Be open to his inspiration, and journal about the fruit that comes from your prayer.

Jesus is looking at you. He asks you a question. What do you say in reply?

What words stood out to you as you prayed?
What did you find stirring in your heart?

_____

_____

_____

_____

_____

_____

_____

_____

_____

_____

_____

_____

_____

_____

_____

_____

_____

_____

_____

_____

_____

Here are three questions to help you reflect on this week's meditations. You may find it helpful to discuss them with others or ponder them on your own before you begin the weekly reflection:

- As we explored this week, it's not a matter of whether we have questions for and about God, but instead *where we go* with the questions (or, rather, *to whom* we go). What questions about Jesus, his Passion, his Church, or your faith have arisen in your heart this week? How is God inviting you to bring those questions back to him in prayer?

- Which individual(s) from this week's readings and reflections stood out to you the most: the ten lepers, the blind beggar, the Apostles, the Pharisees, Zacchaeus, Judas, someone else? Why? How does picturing Jesus' journey from their perspective teach you something more about God, his love, his mercy, and/or your relationship with him?

- **VIDEO REFLECTION:** Throughout Lent, in what ways have you sensed Jesus inviting you to surrender the boundaries and "boxes" in your heart that you have used to keep him out?

Now take a moment to reflect on the past week, going over the meditations that bore the most fruit in your prayer, the things you wrote, and your reflections on this week's video. How has your prayer changed this week?

Unwavering

Implications

"Get away from here, for Herod wants to kill you."

—LUKE 13:31

E arlier in the journey, we read that Jesus "went on his way through towns and villages, teaching, and journeying toward Jerusalem" (Luke 13:22). Soon some Pharisees came to warn him about Herod:

> At that very hour some Pharisees came, and said to him, "Get away from here, for Herod wants to kill you." And he said to them, "Go and tell that fox, 'Behold, I cast out demons and perform cures today and tomorrow, and the third day I finish my course.' ... O Jerusalem, Jerusalem, killing the prophets and stoning those who are sent to you! How often would I have gathered your children together as a hen gathers her brood under her wings, and you would not! Behold, your house is forsaken. And I tell you, you will not see me until you say, 'Blessed is he who comes in the name of the Lord!'" (Luke 13:31–32, 34–35).

"Get away from here, for Herod wants to kill you," they warned him. Now, weeks later, as Jesus prepares to enter Jerusalem, we know he was aware that there were those who wanted to kill him. But notice his earlier response: "Go and tell that fox, 'Behold, I cast out demons and I perform cures today and tomorrow, and the third day I finish my course.'"

Jesus is unmoved by Herod's intimidation. Jesus is unfazed by the conspiracy that confronts him.

There are consequences to loving as Jesus loves. Not everyone is ready for the reality of love. Some choose control over communion. To give ourselves over to love means to let go of control and to trust wholeheartedly in the God who loves us. Some people reject this. Some reject Jesus. And some will reject us because we love

Jesus. Yes, there are consequences to love, especially when love pushes past accepted boundaries, as Jesus' love does.

Jesus is prepared to endure these consequences because of his love for the Father and his love for us. In his mission as the Bridegroom-Messiah, eternity itself is at stake: heaven or hell, salvation or damnation. The Bridegroom has come to save the Bride, and the stakes are enormous.

When Herod threatens to kill Jesus, Jesus knows that the greater threat is to the salvation of mankind. With his eyes on the Father and on the Bride, Jesus accepts the consequences and moves ahead confidently to save us.

For Your Prayer

Stay here for an additional ten minutes. Today pray with Luke 13:22, 31–35. Be present in the scene. Be there with Jesus. Ask the Holy Spirit to help you see what the people in the Gospel saw and hear what they heard. Imagine the scene unfolding as it does in the Bible, but imagine that you are there too. Then, at the end of the scene, imagine that Jesus looks at you. Jesus asks you how you feel about the news of Herod calling for his death. How do you respond?

What words stood out to you as you prayed?
What did you find stirring in your heart?

Passivity

"Do you think that I have come to give peace on earth? No, I tell you, but rather division."

—LUKE 12:51

Earlier in Luke's Gospel, we read about an incident that makes more sense to Jesus' followers as they get closer to Jerusalem. Crowds were growing. Tension was mounting. And as Jesus continued his journey to Jerusalem, many were growing uneasy. The scribes and Pharisees were scandalized and whispered among themselves. The disciples were troubled. The brewing tension was not what they had expected.

Throughout it all, Jesus walked in composed silence, in communion with the Father. Rooted in the Father and afraid of no one, Jesus then rose from his silence and shocked the crowds. He said, "Do you think that I have come to give peace on earth? No, I tell you, but rather division" (Luke 12:51).

Jesus will not avoid conflict when it is necessary. Jesus yearns for his Bride to be free from sin and restored to unfettered communion. Precisely because he loves his Bride, Jesus rejects the notion that he has come to establish peace. He knows that peace is often confused with passivity. Jesus cannot redeem his Bride by remaining passive. He must stay rooted in the truth.

Far too often, we mistake passivity for peace. We don't want to upset the status quo, because doing so might provoke an attack—so we mistake peace for a lack of conflict, while underneath our passivity there remain grave injustices, deep unrest, and fear-filled unforgiveness. It happens at work and at school, at home and in our extended families. It happens in Washington and in the media. We just want everyone to get along.

But passivity ignores truth to ensure that no one is offended. Jesus—the real Jesus—always proclaims the truth. Even when the truth ruffles feathers and causes tension, Jesus cannot *not* speak the truth. He causes division not for division's sake but for the sake of the truth. Passivity is actually sinful if we maintain it at the expense of truth and authentic love.

What is your attitude toward division? What is your attitude toward passivity? How far are you willing to go for the sake of authentic love?

For Your Prayer

Stay here for an additional ten minutes. Today return to the guided meditation from just a few days ago, Saturday of the Fourth Week of Lent. Repeat the meditation, but this time keep Luke 12:51 in your mind. Knowing that there is a difference between peace and passivity, how would you respond to Jesus' question, "Will you promise to stay with me?" What do you say in reply?

What words stood out to you as you prayed?
What did you find stirring in your heart?

Silent

"Is it lawful to heal on the Sabbath, or not?"

—LUKE 14:3

Soon after Jesus tells his disciples that he has come to bring division, he dines on the Sabbath at the house of a ruler of the Pharisees. There he encounters "a man before him who had dropsy," a serious disease marked by swellings. The Pharisees are observing Jesus carefully, so Jesus asks them, "Is it lawful to heal on the Sabbath, or not?" Stunned, the Pharisees have no answer. Scripture says "they were silent" (Luke 14:1–4).

They were *silent*.

Jesus disregards their silence and takes the man with dropsy, heals him, and lets him go (Luke 14:4). Then Jesus presses the point even further. He asks the Pharisees, "Which of you, having a son or an ox that has fallen into a well, will not immediately pull him out on a sabbath day?" (Luke 14:5). If the Pharisees were honest, they probably would have admitted that such an act of mercy—to rescue an animal, or even their own child, from a dangerous situation—would not be an unlawful act. But Luke tells us that, once again, the Pharisees couldn't answer (Luke 14:6).

Jesus pushes the envelope as he heals on the Sabbath in the home of a Pharisee. Confronting their resistance and fear, Jesus cannot be silent when they are silent. The truth of his identity as the Messiah cannot be silenced. The truth of God's mercy cannot be silenced. The truth can never be silenced, regardless of the compartments and categories we construct to help us ignore it.

Compartments keep life neat. Our passivity lets us pretend things are safe. Boxes give us false permission to remain silent. We don't have to struggle; we don't have to challenge anyone. There is no drama, no tension, no confrontation. But mercy—the kind of mercy that changes the world—doesn't live in a box.

Love does not yield to passivity. Jesus cannot, and will not, remain silent when it means denying the Father or his mission to redeem the world.

Love is a person whose name is Jesus Christ. And when you and I fall in love with Jesus, we will do anything for him. When we are in love with Jesus, we will surrender our boxes and no longer remain silent. Whether through words or actions, love demands that we not remain silent.

The Pharisees were silent that day. But love cannot be silent.

For Your Prayer

Stay here for an additional ten minutes. Today pray with Luke 14:1–4. Notice how Jesus is not passive. What is he trying to say to you? How do you respond?

What words stood out to you as you prayed?
What did you find stirring in your heart?

_____

_____

_____

_____

_____

_____

_____

_____

_____

_____

_____

_____

_____

_____

_____

_____

_____

_____

_____

_____

_____

_____

_____

_____

_____

Stone

"He has been dead four days."

—JOHN 11:39*

---

* We are traveling with Jesus using the Gospel of Luke as our map. But the other Gospels also describe Jesus' journey to Jerusalem. This week and next, I have included stories from the other Gospels—not to distract you from the text of Luke, but to help you further appreciate what is happening before and after Jesus' triumphant entrance into Jerusalem.

Before they reach Jerusalem, Jesus is called to the town of Bethany by startling news: his dear friend Lazarus is dying. We will let the Apostle John tell the story.

Lazarus is the brother of Mary and Martha, and his sisters have sent word to Jesus that "he whom you love is ill" (John 11:3). Jesus knows that Lazarus will die, for he says to the Apostles, "Lazarus is dead; and for your sake I am glad that I was not there, so that you may believe" (John 11:14–15). Although death has overtaken Lazarus, Jesus knows the Father's plans for glory. He travels to Bethany knowing well what will soon happen.

"Now when Jesus came, he found that Lazarus had already been in the tomb four days" (John 11:17). Jesus speaks to Martha and Mary and is deeply moved. He weeps, and then he goes with them to Lazarus' tomb. There he boldly commands, "Take away the stone" (John 11:39).

Let me remind you of the circumstances: Lazarus has been dead for days. His body has been sealed in darkness, and nature has begun to take its course. "Martha, the sister of the dead man, said to him, 'Lord, by this time there will be an odor; he has been dead four days'" (John 11:39).

Jesus is not afraid of decay. He is not afraid of the stench or the mess. He stands at the entrance of the tomb and proclaims, "Lazarus, come out" (John 11:43). And the dead man emerges from the dark tomb. Lazarus is alive. He is free. Lazarus walks out of the tomb, out of the darkness and back into life.

The event reveals Jesus' power over death, of course, and points to his upcoming resurrection from the dead. But for a moment, let us also appreciate the Master's authority over the darkness and the tomb.

As I've said before, many of us have things in our life that we keep hidden away in the dark. We have our own buried secrets, and most of us are afraid of them. We keep our hearts closed, like the entrance to Lazarus' tomb. Inside, in our fear, the darkness deepens. When Jesus says, "Take away the stone," we may resist, seeking to keep the tomb of our heart closed. Why?

Deacon James Keating writes, "With ever more accurate darts of love the Holy Spirit opens our consciences before God so that deeper and more effective healing can occur; at times His coming is so pure that it causes us to have pain and recoil at the level of intimacy God wishes His Son to achieve in our being. We recoil at our own needed medicine because it will bring about a change, and sin wishes no change to occur."[12] In other words, when God gets too close to our stench, we recoil and push him away out of fear.

Do not be afraid! Jesus is not afraid of the tomb. He simply asks us to take away the stone—to open our hearts so that he may free us from the darkness inside.

For Your Prayer

Stay here for an additional ten minutes. Today pray with John 11:1–44. Be present in the scene. Be there with Jesus. Ask the Holy Spirit to help you see what the people in the Gospel saw and hear what they heard. Be with Jesus as he calls Lazarus out of the tomb. What stirs within you? What do you desire?

What words stood out to you as you prayed?
What did you find stirring in your heart?

Allow

"From that day on they planned to kill him."

—JOHN 11:53 NAB

L azarus' resurrection causes a ripple effect. Everyone is stunned. Word spreads like wildfire, and many Jews who had seen what he did believed in him (John 11:45). However, even as the glory of God is made manifest in Bethany, evil abounds and conspiracy lurks. We read that "some of them went to the Pharisees and told them what Jesus had done" (John 11:46).

Threatened by Jesus' popularity, the Pharisees and chief priests call for a meeting of the Sanhedrin, the supreme religious council, to decide what to do. They are afraid that if they let Jesus go on like this, "every one will believe in him, and the Romans will come and destroy both our holy place and our nation" (John 11:48).

Selfish shadows loom as Caiaphas, the high priest, presses in and prophesies, "It is better for you that one man should die instead of the people, so that the whole nation may not perish" (John 11:50 NAB).

It has been spoken now. It has been said. It is set in motion. A plot—a conspiracy—murder. For "from that day on they took counsel about how to put him to death" (John 11:53). They will murder him. They will hunt him down. Jesus—this Jesus with whom you have journeyed, with whom you have fallen in love—is now a wanted man, for they mean to kill him.

The scribes and Pharisees are now plotting to kill Jesus, and the Father allows it to happen. Of course, we know that Jesus freely gives his life, for he himself said, "I lay down my life ... no one takes it from me, but I lay it down of my own accord" (John 10:17–18). While Jesus freely gives his life, the Father allows the conspiracy to unfold. Why? Why does God allow things like this to happen?

Let us once again steep ourselves in the quote from yesterday: "With ever more accurate darts of love the Holy Spirit opens our consciences before God so that deeper and more effective healing can occur; at times His coming is so pure that it causes us to have pain and recoil at the level of intimacy God wishes His Son to achieve in our being. We recoil at our own needed medicine because it will bring about a change, and sin wishes no change to occur."[13]

We can push back against God. We can resist God. We can reject God. When God seeks to touch the deepest areas of our fear-driven control, we can recoil from him. For his part, God never forces himself on us. He constantly invites, but he never coerces. He never stops trying, but he never manipulates. God allows us to say yes or no because he reverences our free will. Even when there are consequences to such love, God allows the "no" because, without free will, there will never be the ultimate "yes."

For Your Prayer

Stay here for an additional ten minutes. Today pray with John 11:54–57. Be present in the scene. Ask the Holy Spirit to help you see what the people in the Gospel saw and hear what they heard. What's in your heart as they talk about conspiracy?

What words stood out to you as you prayed?
What did you find stirring in your heart?

Surrender

*"No one takes [my life] from me, but I
lay it down of my own accord.
I have power to lay it down, and I have
power to take it again; this charge I
have received from my Father."*

—JOHN 10:18

Pope Benedict XVI once wrote, "There is a certain relationship between love and the Divine ... a reality far greater and totally other than our everyday existence. Yet we have also seen that the way to attain this goal is not simply by submitting to instinct. Purification and growth in maturity are called for; and these also pass through the path of renunciation."[14]

The Holy Father is saying that love must be purified if it is to mature. We must be purified if we are going to love well. This requires renunciation, which is self-denial or surrender.

Pope Benedict XVI continues,

> Love is ... not in the sense of a moment of intoxication, but rather as a journey, an ongoing exodus out of the closed inward-looking self towards its liberation through self-giving, and thus towards authentic self-discovery and indeed the discovery of God: "Whoever seeks to gain his life will lose it, but whoever loses his life will preserve it" (Luke 17:33), as Jesus says throughout the Gospels. ... In these words, Jesus portrays his own path, which leads through the Cross to the Resurrection: the path of the grain of wheat that falls to the ground and dies, and in this way bears much fruit. Starting from the depths of his own sacrifice and of the love that reaches fulfillment therein, he also portrays in these words the essence of love and indeed of human life itself.[15]

If love—real love—is a response to the love God has for us, then our inevitable response to God is surrender. God is God; we are not. His love is so pure that the only appropriate response to it is to receive it, to surrender. Surrender is "an ongoing exodus out of the closed inward-looking self" so that our life is about God.

This surrender is found in the everyday. What Pope Benedict XVI once said to priests really applies to all of us: "In the words 'I do,' spoken at our priestly ordination, we made this fundamental renunciation of our desire to be independent, 'self-made.' But day by day this great 'yes' has to be lived out in the many little 'yeses' and small sacrifices. This 'yes' made up of tiny steps, which together make up the great 'yes,' can be lived out without bitterness and self-pity only if Christ is truly the center of our lives."[16]

Jesus surrendered long before he entered Jerusalem or knelt to pray in the Garden of Gethsemane. Jesus lived in perfect communion with the Father, in perfect surrender to the Father's will. Day by day, Jesus' great "yes" was lived out in many little "yeses" and small sacrifices. In freedom, pure freedom, Jesus chooses what awaits him in Jerusalem because Jesus has lived in perfect surrender every day.

For Your Prayer

Stay here for an additional ten minutes. Today pray with the third quote from Pope Benedict XVI mentioned above: "In the words 'I do'..." What strikes you? What and how do you need to surrender to God?

What words stood out to you as you prayed?
What did you find stirring in your heart?

_____

_____

_____

_____

_____

_____

_____

_____

_____

_____

_____

_____

_____

_____

_____

_____

_____

_____

_____

_____

_____

_____

Fast

"I proclaimed a fast ... that we might humble ourselves before our God ... "

—EZRA 8:21

We all love new things: new clothes, a new car, a new phone or tablet, a new show or book. And in our "on-demand" society, we can usually get ahold of such things in no time at all. Rarely do any of us have to wait—to hunger—for anything, at least not for very long.

But sometimes, in our pursuit of all things new, we lose sight of what is time-honored and precious from the past. And sometimes, thanks to instant gratification, we forget that some things are worth hungering for.

This is why fasting is so important. Fasting is a precious tradition of the past. It has deep spiritual and scriptural roots. My good friend Fr. Josh Johnson explains how fasting can be considered the very first commandment in the Bible: specifically in Genesis 2:17, when God asked Adam not to eat—in other words, to fast—from the fruit of the Tree of the Knowledge of Good and Evil.[17]

More than that, as a spiritual discipline, fasting is very powerful. By practicing self-denial, we can break free from the things and habits which steal our attention away from God. By saying "no" to the flesh, we can say "yes" to the eternal and respond to the movements of the Spirit within us. By experiencing physical hunger, we can better recognize our spiritual hunger for God, our need for intimacy with him.

If you are unfamiliar with fasting as a spiritual practice, I invite you to discover it now. Fasting can produce abundant fruit in our spiritual lives and have a profound effect on our ability to be more receptive to God.

So, to prepare you for Holy Week, I am going to ask you to do something I've asked members of the *Lenten Companion* community to do before—and will ask you to do again. Some of us may have already been going without a favorite food during Lent, like chocolate, candy, or snacks. In addition to those fasts, I invite you to fast in three distinct ways from now to Easter Sunday:

1. Fast from using your smartphone. Before you reject this idea entirely, ask yourself: When is the last time you used your smartphone as just a phone? Let's be honest, how much time do we actually use our phones to distract or entertain ourselves? I'm not asking you to ignore your phone or turn it off. But, at least for next week—the holiest of weeks—reserve using your smartphone only for *essential* phone calls, emails, or text messages. Fasting from your smartphone will mean putting it on silent: no apps, no internet, no social media. You will find that it takes discipline and prayer to fast from these distractions.

2. Fast from noise. This means no radio, no television, no music, no optional noise. Instead, intentionally choose and cultivate silence. Exterior silence helps us become open to interior silence. I promise that you will discover two things in the silence. One, you will realize just how distracting the everyday noise in your life really is; and two, you will learn to recognize the quiet and subtle voice of God, who is always speaking to you but usually has to compete with all the noise.

3. Fast from food and alcohol. This means no alcohol from now to Easter Sunday. It also means (for healthy individuals with no medical exceptions) limiting what you eat every day to the amount you would normally eat in just two meals combined— and no snacking. Eating less creates a hunger within us, and as I mentioned already, physical hunger deepens our spiritual hunger. In this way, we can create more space in our hearts for God to dwell.

These requests may seem extreme. They may make you uncomfortable. Fasting itself is an uncomfortable practice—but from that discomfort, we have a real chance to draw closer to God in a way we rarely experience in our day-to-day lives. Let's not forget, Holy Week is not like any other week: it is *the* week. And, if I may be brutally honest, fasting for one week from your phone and noise and alcohol and a little food seems like a small sacrifice compared to how much God has sacrificed for us.

For Your Prayer

Stay here for an additional ten minutes. Today read and pray with the Gospel for the Procession with Palms (which you will hear tomorrow on Palm Sunday), Mark 11:1–10. Ask the Holy Spirit to help you see what the people in the crowd saw and hear what they heard. Imagine the scene unfolding as it does in the Bible, but imagine that you too are there in the crowd. What stirs within you? What will help you welcome the Lord and stay close to him this week?

What words stood out to you as you prayed?
What did you find stirring in your heart?

Here are three questions to help you reflect on this week's meditations. You may find it helpful to discuss them with others or ponder them on your own before you begin the weekly reflection:

- Pope Benedict XVI teaches us that, to give God our full, absolute "yes," we must begin by giving him our many little "yeses" and small daily sacrifices. In what area(s) of your life can you try to offer God more of your little "yeses"? What places in your heart is God waiting for you to surrender to him so that healing and new growth can take place?

- As we reflected on yesterday, fasting can be challenging—but the best way to succeed in a challenge is to have a plan. To prepare for Holy Week, what steps can you take now to help yourself fast from (or at least strictly limit) using your smartphone, excess noise, and food and alcohol? Who will hold you accountable?

- **VIDEO REFLECTION:** Follow Fr. Toups as he leads you in the guided meditation in this video. What strikes you the most as you imagine this scene? How do you feel this moment launching you into Holy Week?

Now take a moment to reflect on the past week, going over the meditations that bore the most fruit in your prayer, the things you wrote, and your reflections on this week's video. How has your prayer changed this week?

Faithful

Lamb

"Blessed is the King who comes in the name of the Lord! Peace in heaven and glory in the highest!"

—LUKE 19:38

The time has come. We are here. Behold, Jerusalem! The city is full of people, for Jews from all over Israel have come to celebrate the Passover. And now Jesus' epic, life-changing journey has come to this day, this most sacred day.

Welcome to Palm Sunday. "And as he rode along, they spread their garments on the road. As he was now drawing near, at the descent of the Mount of Olives, the whole multitude of the disciples began to rejoice and praise God with a loud voice for all the mighty works that they had seen, saying, 'Blessed is the King who comes in the name of the Lord! Peace in heaven and glory in the highest!'" (Luke 19:36–38).

Why did Jesus enter Jerusalem on Sunday? After all, the Jewish Sabbath is Saturday. And the Passover was on the day we call Holy Thursday. So why did he enter the city on Sunday?

Let us start with John the Baptist. In John 1 we read, "The next day he saw Jesus coming toward him, and said, 'Behold, the Lamb of God, who takes away the sin of the world!'" (John 1:29). Then, soon after, we read, "The next day again John was standing with two of his disciples; and he looked at Jesus as he walked, and said, 'Behold, the Lamb of God!'" (John 1:35–37).

John the Baptist knows that Jesus is the Messiah, so why does he refer to him as the Lamb?

In the Old Testament, Exodus 12, we read how God liberated his people from slavery in Egypt, setting them free and eventually leading them to the Promised Land. As the Israelites prepared to leave Egypt, Moses instructed each family to sacrifice a spotless lamb in worship and mark their doorposts with its blood. That night, the homes marked with blood were spared from the final plague, the death of Egypt's firstborn. This was the original Passover event, when God passed over the Israelites' homes, sparing them from death. The blood of the Passover lambs was the price of their freedom.

In Jesus, there is a new covenant and a new Passover. Jesus is the new Passover Lamb. In the new Passover, we are all set free from the slavery of sin. In the new Passover, Jesus, the spotless Lamb, is offered in sacrifice, and his Blood—the Blood of the Lamb of God—is what sets us free.

Exodus 12 gives explicit, detailed, sacred instructions as to when and how the Jews were to eat the Passover meal. One instruction was that each family was to find their spotless lamb five days before the Passover. Thus, before Passover, more than a million Jews descended on Jerusalem. Five days prior to Passover, they were all looking for their lambs.

Jesus enters Jerusalem five days prior to Passover, on the day everyone was looking for a lamb. And in a sense, he says, "Behold, I am the Lamb." They were all looking for a lamb, and Jesus is what they are ultimately looking for.

For Your Prayer

Stay here for an additional ten minutes. Today pray with Luke 19:28–40. Be present in the scene. Be there with Jesus. Ask the Holy Spirit to help you see what the people in the Gospel saw and hear what they heard. Imagine the scene unfolding as it does in the Bible, but imagine that you too are there in the crowd. What stirs within you?

What words stood out to you as you prayed?
What did you find stirring in your heart?

Focused

"He entered the temple … "

—LUKE 19:45

Today as we wrap up the last days of Lent, I would like to lead you in a guided meditation. Let us begin by asking the Holy Spirit to awaken our spiritual senses as we pray. May we receive the gift to see what those in the Gospel saw, to hear what they heard, and to feel what they felt.

Imagine everything that is happening in Jerusalem in preparation for Passover. More than one million people have arrived in the city. The annual pilgrimage festival always brings with it a heightened sense of anticipation, and Jesus' triumphant entrance has added to that. Everywhere you go, everyone is asking if the time has come. Could Jesus really be the Messiah?

Everyone is preparing for Thursday's Passover meal as prescribed in the Scriptures. Houses are being cleaned. Lambs are being prepared. Pilgrims who live outside Jerusalem are celebrating with family members who live in the city. Children are running around, playing with their cousins. Relatives are sharing stories about everything that has happened since they last saw each other.

You have risen early, before anyone else. You look for Jesus but cannot find him where you and the others are staying. Remembering his love for the Temple, you walk there looking for him.

As you arrive in the Temple, you are once again reminded of the glory of God as you take in the majestic interior. You go further inside, and from afar you see Jesus alone, praying. As you approach with great reverence, Jesus senses your presence. He turns to you and smiles.

Jesus seems different today. There is an air of special intensity about him. He seems to be in deep union with the Father and very focused on the present moment.

As you sit beside him, Jesus looks you in the eyes. He is at peace, but he is focused. He feels the immense love of a Bridegroom for his Bride. He feels the love that a Savior has for his people. Jesus' gaze into your eyes pierces your heart.

You are there now. Jesus is looking at you. He is focused on you. Be still. Let him look at you as you look at him. Let him focus on you as you focus on him.

For Your Prayer

Stay here for an additional ten minutes. Reread the guided meditation above, and then close your eyes to imagine yourself in the scene. Do not read along with the book, but instead allow the Holy Spirit to let you experience these moments with the Lord. What are you feeling? What do you want to say to him?

What words stood out to you as you prayed?
What did you find stirring in your heart?

House

"He entered the temple and began to drive out those who sold, saying to them, 'It is written, "My house shall be a house of prayer"; but you have made it a den of robbers.'"

—LUKE 19:45–46

In yesterday's guided meditation, we dwelled with Jesus in prayer in the heart of the Temple early in the morning as the city prepared for Thursday's Passover. Today, we will once again return to the Temple—and things are about to heat up.

Jesus has arrived triumphantly in Jerusalem, and the Temple is one of his first stops. Jesus and his disciples approach the Temple, the only place where a person could come to approach God. As the Apostles walk closely behind Jesus up the Temple steps, they likely wonder whether he would stop to teach. But Jesus has other plans.

We can only imagine the shock of Peter, Matthew, Judas, and the other Apostles as their Master starts driving out the merchants and flipping the money-changers' tables (Matthew 21:12). Coins clatter on the stones as they scatter to the ground. The pigeons, sheep, and oxen being sold for sacrifice are squawking, bleating, and bellowing at all the commotion. Jesus has turned the place completely upside-down.

But the Bridegroom is cleaning house for his Bride—and this space where the merchants had set up shop carries special significance. The merchants had set up shop in the Court of the Gentiles, which was supposed to be reserved for non-Jews to come and offer prayers and thanksgiving to the Lord—but in Jesus' time, the chief priests allowed the merchants to move from outside the Temple into that space. But Jesus wants his house to be a house of prayer for *all* peoples; the Bridegroom wants to restore the union between God and *all* humanity.[18]

Jesus isn't only after the merchants. These sellers and money-changers were only there because the chief priests allowed it. The selling of animals for sacrifice, along with tithes and religious taxes, was a lucrative business for the Temple leaders.[19] By driving the sellers out, Jesus is indirectly calling out the chief priests for prioritizing the wrong thing, condemning them for turning a house of prayer into a "den of robbers" (Luke 19:46).

As if the situation between Jesus and the Pharisees wasn't tense enough! We can only imagine the outrage of the scribes and chief priests. When they heard what Jesus had done, they "sought a way to destroy him" (Mark 11:18).

But Jesus will not be stopped. Jesus—the true owner of the house—has come to set things in order. Soon we will see how those surrounding Jesus will respond to his housecleaning.

For Your Prayer

Stay here for an additional ten minutes. Today read Psalm 69:6–9. Put the words of the psalmist in the context of Jesus cleansing the Temple; imagine Jesus speaking these words to the Father as the chief priests, scribes, and Pharisees seek a way to destroy him. What thoughts stir in your heart?

What words stood out to you as you prayed?
What did you find stirring in your heart?

Agape

*"Judas Iscariot went to the chief priests and said,
'What will you give me if I deliver him to you?'"*

—MATTHEW 26:14–15

Things are moving fast. Each of the Apostles is feeling the intensity of Jesus' cleansing of the Temple and his scathing confrontation with the Pharisees. Peter is stirred by the confrontation and conspiracy. Matthew is troubled by how serious the disputes have become. And Judas—poor Judas—is more confused than anyone.

We don't know why Judas betrays Jesus. We can imagine that Judas had a romantic idea of what would happen in Jerusalem. The palm branches and hosannas only confirmed what he had hoped: that Jesus would enter Jerusalem and be recognized by all as the long-awaited Davidic ruler. But things are quickly unraveling. Powerful scribes hate Jesus. Powerful Pharisees hate Jesus. Members of the Sanhedrin hate Jesus. Judas thinks he loves Jesus, but Judas only loves what he wants Jesus to be.

We can imagine how Judas loves his own ambitions. Judas' "love" for Jesus is self-serving. It is selfish and conditional. It isn't about surrender; it's about Judas.

Dazed, confused, and resentful that things aren't going his way, Judas "went to the chief priests and said, 'What will you give me if I deliver him to you?'" (Matthew 26:14–15).

Let's contrast Judas with Jesus. How does Jesus love? Pope Benedict XVI writes, "Of the three Greek words for love, *eros, philia* (the love of friendship) and *agape*, New Testament writers prefer the last."[20] God's *agape* is a "love which forgives."[21] God is love—and God's love is *agape*. It is a complete gift. There are no strings attached.

We can imagine that Judas betrays Jesus because he is confused, but that confusion is fueled by one thing and one thing only:

Judas' refusal to surrender. Judas' love for Jesus has morphed into a self-serving narcissism because Judas couldn't respond to Jesus with surrender.

For Judas, following Christ is still what Benedict XVI called just "an ethical choice or a lofty idea."[22] Judas' "love" is conditional.

Jesus' love, by contrast, is pure *agape*. It is unconditional. Jesus knows that Judas will betray him. Jesus still invites him to Jerusalem; he still washes Judas' feet in the Upper Room; he still prays with Judas at the Last Supper. Always imbued with *agape*, Jesus keeps reaching out to Judas to the very end. That's love. That's *agape*. That's the love—*agape* love—that Jesus has for you.

For Your Prayer

Stay here for an additional ten minutes. Today pray with Matthew 26:1–16. Be present in the scene. Ask the Holy Spirit to help you see what the people in the Gospel saw and hear what they heard. What's in your heart as Judas makes plans to betray Jesus?

What words stood out to you as you prayed?
What did you find stirring in your heart?

Communion

"This is my body which is given for you."

—LUKE 22:19

Holy Thursday

The Passover ritual was so sacred that from its very institution, God gave instructions: "This day shall be for you a memorial day, and you shall keep it as a feast to the Lord; throughout your generations you shall observe it as an ordinance forever" (Exodus 12:14). Failure to celebrate the Passover properly would result in being "cut off from the congregation of Israel" (Exodus 12:19). Furthermore, the seder (the ceremonial Passover meal) had a script. God was the author of the script, and you never strayed from the script. God was the author, and only God could edit.

As a rabbi, it is Jesus' role to lead his Apostles in the Passover seder meal. Thus, on the night of what we call Holy Thursday, Jesus celebrated the Last Supper, the Passover ritual meal, with them. As the leader, Jesus is supposed to re-present the sacred Passover text recounting the story of the Exodus from Egypt. As he does this, Jesus fulfills the Passover celebration established in Exodus 12 when he institutes the Eucharist. Finishing the seder script, he takes the piece of unleavened bread and says, "This is my body which is given for you" (Luke 22:19).

This is my body, which I give for you. This kind of language easily calls to mind another type of celebration: marriage. Marriage involves a total self-gift and intimate union between a bridegroom and bride. As the Bridegroom who has come for his Bride, Jesus longs for the fullness of a marriage with humanity—and, as we remember through the Eucharist, he offers us a gift of his entire self: body, blood, soul, and divinity.

John Paul II once wrote that "Christ is the Bridegroom because 'he has given himself': his body has been 'given,' his blood has been 'poured out.' ... The 'sincere gift' contained in the Sacrifice of the Cross gives definitive prominence to the spousal meaning of God's love. As the Redeemer of the world, Christ is the Bridegroom of the Church. *The Eucharist is the Sacrament of our Redemption. It is the Sacrament of the Bridegroom and of the Bride.*"[23]

As the spotless Lamb of God, Jesus' sacrifice takes away the sins of the world. As the Bridegroom, Jesus' self-gift redeems the relationship with his Bride, once broken in the Fall. The Eucharist truly is Jesus—his body, blood, soul, and divinity—which he gives freely for our sake.

The Eucharist nourishes us in body and soul and draws us into deeper union with the Bridegroom-Messiah, Jesus. As members of his mystical body, the Church, we are invited to participate in this one-flesh union with Jesus whenever we receive Holy Communion.

For Your Prayer

If possible, attend tonight's Holy Thursday Mass. If you need to, celebrate the Sacrament of Reconciliation before Mass. As you hear the priest echo Jesus' words—"This is my body which is given for you"—reflect on how Jesus is offering his very body, blood, soul, and divinity. As you receive the Eucharist, dwell on how Jesus is inviting you into intimate communion with him.

What words stood out to you as you prayed?
What did you find stirring in your heart?

Commit

*"Father, into your hands
I commit my spirit!"*

—LUKE 23:46

Good Friday

Yesterday, we dwelled on the Eucharist, the total self-gift of Jesus in body, blood, soul, and divinity. Today, on this most solemn of days, Jesus truly fulfills the words he spoke during the Last Supper: "This is my body, given for you."

Things move very quickly after the Passover meal with his Apostles. A lonely evening in the Garden of Gethsemane is followed by betrayal, arrest, accusations, scourging, mockery, and finally a death sentence. Jesus is forced to carry a device of torture all the way to the outskirts of the city, where only a few faithful souls stand by amid a taunting crowd.

The chief priests, scribes, and elders start: "He saved others; let him save himself, if he is the Christ of God, his Chosen One!" The heckling soldiers join in: "If you are the King of the Jews, save yourself!" Even one of the men executed with him joins in: "Are you not the Christ? Save yourself and us!" (Luke 23: 35, 37, 39).

Why? Why doesn't Jesus save himself? Why won't he use his divine power and come down from the Cross? Why not prove to the doubters once and for all that he is the Christ, the Son of God?

The answer goes back to the very start of Lent. At the very beginning of the season, we read about how Jesus was "resolutely determined" to journey to Jerusalem (Luke 9:51 NAB). He is *fully committed*. During this whole journey, he would not let death threats, conspiracy, or betrayal turn him from his course. Not even a painful, humiliating death would stop him from loving us to the full.

Love is something you *do*. Jesus performs this act of love on the Cross for everyone: Jew and Gentile, Pharisee and tax collector, John and Judas, those who love him and those who abandoned him. His love for all these—and for me, and for *you*—is relentless, passionate, and limitless. His love will not falter, not until the holy reunion between God and man, Bridegroom and Bride, is accomplished.

So, fully committed, Jesus completes his task: "Father, into your hands I commit my spirit!"

And, with one last breath, it is finished.

For Your Prayer

Stay here for an additional ten minutes. Today pray with the Passion narrative from the Gospel of John (John 18:1–19:42, which will be read at today's Good Friday service). Be present in the scene. Be there with Jesus. Ask the Holy Spirit to help you see what the people in the Gospel saw and hear what they heard. Imagine the scene unfolding as it does in the Bible, but imagine that you are there too as Jesus is crucified. Then, from the Cross, Jesus looks at you. How do you respond in your heart?

What words stood out to you as you prayed?
What did you find stirring in your heart?

Shroud

*"Joseph took the body, and wrapped
it in a clean linen shroud ... "*

—MATTHEW 27:59

Holy Saturday

It is finished. Jesus' journey to Jerusalem has ended. His body lies in the tomb of Joseph of Arimathea, covered in a shroud, hidden behind a heavy stone slab.

To everyone who knew Jesus—those who followed him, who loved him, who were challenged by him, who reviled him—it would seem his story is over. The spectacle of the crucifixion has ended; the crowds disperse, and only a handful of souls remain to lay Jesus to rest. As Jesus goes into the tomb, "there is a great silence on earth ... a great silence and stillness. The whole earth keeps silence because the King is asleep."[24]

The world is shrouded in silence just as Jesus is shrouded in the tomb. This simple linen burial cloth covers his wounds and hides his body from sight. The shroud serves as a curtain, a barrier, marking the border between the living from the dead. Now that the shroud is wrapped around Jesus, he has truly crossed the threshold into death, into the loneliest place of all human experience.

But here is the paradoxical mystery of Holy Saturday: Life itself enters death. As Benedict XVI wrote, "God, having made himself man, reached the point of entering man's most extreme and absolute solitude ... Even in the extreme darkness of the most absolute human loneliness we may hear a voice that calls us and find a hand that takes ours and leads us out."[25]

In the shroud of Jesus, stained with the blood of his sacrifice, we see "not only darkness but also the light; not so much the defeat of life and of love, but rather victory, the victory of life over death, of love over hatred."[26]

In this final stage of his journey as the Bridegroom-Messiah, Jesus shows us there is no place where his redemptive love and mercy cannot reach. There is no darkness in this world where his light cannot shine. There is no loneliness we could ever experience where he does not dwell with us. Not even the darkness and loneliness of the tomb can hold off the power of the Resurrection.

Today, in this space between Christ's Passion and the victory of Easter, we can imagine the Bridegroom saying: "The bridal chamber is adorned, the banquet is ready, the eternal dwelling places are prepared, the treasure houses of all good things lie open. The kingdom of heaven has been prepared for you from all eternity."[27]

For Your Prayer

Stay here for an additional ten minutes. Today pray with Matthew 27:57–61. Be present in the scene. Ask the Holy Spirit to help you see what the people in the Gospel saw and hear what they heard. Imagine the scene unfolding as it does in the Bible, but imagine that you too are there, outside the tomb where Jesus lay. Stay awhile with the women who sit opposite Christ's tomb. Rest in the profound silence of Holy Saturday.

What words stood out to you as you prayed?
What did you find stirring in your heart?

Remember

"And they remembered his words ... "

—LUKE 24:8

Easter Sunday

Our Lenten journey to Jerusalem has also been a journey through the Gospel of Luke. It would therefore be appropriate today for us to receive the gift of Easter through Luke's account of the Resurrection.

We read in Luke 24:1: "On the first day of the week, at early dawn, they went to the tomb." We can only imagine what would have been in these disciples' hearts as they "went to the tomb." Because of their encounter with Jesus, their lives had been changed. They had hope. They had tasted God's mercy. They saw themselves, and all of life, differently. Then, suddenly, the storm of betrayal and Jesus' traumatic scourging and crucifixion invaded their newfound spiritual growth. The rollercoaster of events from Palm Sunday to Holy Thursday and Good Friday would have been emotionally distressing and spiritually exhausting.

Now imagine these disciples arriving at Jesus' tomb and finding "the stone rolled away" (Luke 24:2) and angels declaring that "He is not here, but has risen" (Luke 24:5). Scripture says that the disciples were "perplexed" (Luke 24:4), and the awe of the moment was so powerful that "they were frightened and bowed their faces to the ground" (Luke 24:5). Then, at last, everything clicked when "they remembered his words" (Luke 24:8).

All of their emotions, confusion, and desolation were shattered *when they remembered his words.*

You and I have much in common with the disciples of Luke's Resurrection narrative. Because of our encounter with Jesus, our lives have been changed. We have hope. We have tasted God's mercy. We now see ourselves, and all of life, differently. However, similarly to the disciples, we too experience the ebb and flow of spiritual consolation and spiritual desolation. Throughout all our ups and downs in the spiritual life, it's vital for us to "remember his words."

The question that hovered over the disciples as they walked to the tomb was "What's next?" The reality of Jesus' risen presence provided direction amidst their next chapter of discipleship. Many of us reading today may be asking the same question: "What's next?" To you, my friend, I say: *Remember his words.*

This Lent has been less about a book and more about a person— Jesus. The same Jesus who rose on Easter Sunday and led his disciples is the same Jesus who is risen today, who wants to lead *you.* What will help you most going forward is to remember the words he has said to you thus far on the journey.

In the coming weeks, I encourage you to reread your journal. Return to pages that spoke to you. Revisit meditations that may still have more for you to receive. Whenever you can't hear his voice or what he is saying, remember the words he has already spoken, knowing that those words are timeless and forever new.

Be not afraid. He is risen. He is leading you. All you have to do is "remember his words."

For Your Prayer

Stay here for an additional ten minutes. Today review your journal and the previous mediations. Ask yourself: "What was the theme of this Lent? What did God say to me? What is he saying to me now?"

What words stood out to you as you prayed?
What did you find stirring in your heart?

Easter

*"Weeping may last for the night,
but joy comes with the morning."*

—PSALM 30:5

Endnotes

1. Benedict XVI, *Deus Caritas Est* (December 25, 2005), 1, emphasis added.

2. Ignatius of Loyola, "Contemplation to Attain Love of God," *The Spiritual Exercises of St. Ignatius*, trans. Louis J. Puhl, S.J. (Chicago: Loyola Press, 1951), 234 (p. 102).

3. Benedict XVI, *Deus Caritas Est*, 2.

4. Thomas Aquinas, *Summa Theologica* (*ST*) I–II.26.4.

5. Christopher West, *Theology of the Body Explained: A Commentary on John Paul II's Man and Woman He Created Them* (Boston: Pauline Books and Media, 2007), 60.

6. West, 60.

7. West, 60.

8. John Paul II, *Letter to Families* (February 2, 1994), 18.

9. "The Order of Celebrating Matrimony Within Mass," *The Order of Celebrating Matrimony: The Roman Ritual*, 2nd ed. (Collegeville: Liturgical Press, 2016), 60.

10. *The Order of Celebrating Matrimony*, 62.

11. Augustine of Hippo, *The Confessions of St. Augustine*, ed. Rosalie De Rosset (Chicago: Moody Publishers, 2007), I.1.3.

12. James Keating, "The Healing Power of the Eucharist," December 6, 2021, St. Paul Center for Biblical Theology, stpaulcenter.com.

13. Keating.

14. Benedict XVI, *Deus Caritas Est*, 5.

15. Benedict XVI, 6.

16. Benedict XVI, Chrism Mass homily (April 9, 2009), vatican.va.

17. Joshua Johnson, "Dealing with Depression or Acedia in Lent, Types of Fasting, and Distractions in Prayer," podcast, 14:36, *Ask Fr. Josh: Your Catholic Question and Answer Podcast,* Ascension, February 18, 2021, spotify.com.

18. Marcellino D'Ambrosio, *Jesus: The Way, the Truth, and the Life* (West Chester, PA: Ascension, 2020), 201–202.

19. D'Ambrosio, 201.

20. Benedict XVI, *Deus Caritas Est,* 3.

21. Benedict XVI, 10.

22. Benedict XVI, 1.

23. John Paul II, *Mulieris Dignitatem* (1988), 26, emphasis in original.

24. "From an Ancient Homily for Holy Saturday," from the *Patrologia Graeca* (43, 439, 451, 462–463), in *Liturgy of the Hours,* trans. ICEL (New York: Catholic Book Publishing, 1976), 2.496.

25. Benedict XVI, "Pastoral Visit to Turin: Veneration of the Holy Shroud in the Cathedral of Turin" (May 2, 2010), vatican.va.

26. Benedict XVI, "Pastoral Visit to Turin."

27. "Ancient Homily for Holy Saturday," 2.498.

CREDITS

Executive Producer
Jonathan Strate

General Manager
Jeffrey Cole, Lauren McCann

Product Manager and Content Manager
Julia Coppa Bernetsky, Lauren Welsh

Project Manager
Veronica Salazar

Editorial
Rebecca Robinson, Christina Eberle

Graphics
Stella Ziegler, Sarah Stueve

Video
Matt Pirrall, Ellie Spencer, Worklight Pictures

Marketing
Mark Leopold, Julia Morgensai

ABOUT THE AUTHOR

 Ordained in 2001, Fr. Mark Toups is known for his joyful, encouraging spiritual advice as he helps Catholics develop habits of daily prayer. His many books and studies with Ascension serve as valued resources for Catholics to deepen their prayer lives and encounter the Lord in meaningful ways, particularly through meditation on the Scriptures and through celebration of the seasons of Advent and Lent.

Fr. Toups is a priest for the Diocese of Houma-Thibodaux, where he is the pastor of Our Lady of the Isle in Grand Isle, Louisiana. In addition to his pastoral work, Fr. Toups is an adjunct faculty member for the Institute for Priestly Formation, specializing in communications, development, and spiritual direction. Fr. Toups received his Master of Divinity (MDiv) degree from Notre Dame Seminary in New Orleans. A graduate of Nicholls State University, he is a native of Houma, Louisiana.

Fr. Toups is the author of *Oremus: A Catholic Guide to Prayer*, the *Rejoice!* Advent Meditations series, and *The Ascension Lenten Companion* series.

ABOUT THE ILLUSTRATOR

Mike Moyers has illustrated *Rejoice!* and *The Ascension Lenten Companion* since both series began six years ago, capturing in them the beauty and wonder of the lives of Jesus, Mary, and Joseph and those they loved. His paintings present the Holy Family and other figures from Scripture in a more human way so they no longer feel like characters in a story but real people. "We are witnesses of God's wonders," he says.

Mike begins a painting by reading and praying with a Bible story, imagining the details. Then, he says, "I have to let God take it from there." His paintings thus often capture the in-between moments of familiar stories—quiet and tender gestures that we know must have happened along the way. He purposely keeps some details vague to make space for the Holy Spirit, so what we see can be shaped by a deeper vision. His hope is "that people will continue to enjoy and receive God's grace through the paintings I make."

He lives with his wife and children in Franklin, Tennessee. See more of his work at mikemoyersfineart.com.

Learn more about Mike's journey and the faith that inspires him: